SACRED
SISTERING

A DEVOTIONAL FOR WOMEN OF COLOR MINISTRY LEADERS

RISE Together Mentorship Network

SACRED
SISTERING

A DEVOTIONAL FOR WOMEN OF COLOR MINISTRY LEADERS

VINE
PUBLISHING

TO:

_____

FROM:

_____

DATE:

_____

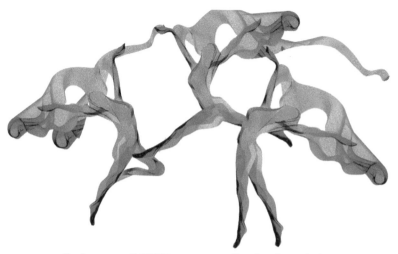

In honor of OUR women of color in ministry,

Pioneers and Trailblazers

whose voices were silenced,

religious leadership opportunities limited,

and yet,

their SPIRITS soared

leaving us a legacy of Sacred Sistering

and

making a way for each of us to RISE Together.

ACKNOWLEDGEMENTS

I am extremely appreciative of how the spirit of God has touched and inspired many persons and institutions to support and bring the vision of a Sacred Sistering devotional to fulfillment. Without the Grace of God and funding support from the Lilly Endowment Inc., this Thriving in Ministry writing project would not have been possible. A special thank you to Chris Coble, Senior Vice President of Religion and Jessicah Duckworth, Program Director. Their ongoing support throughout the planning, implementation, and sustainability phases of the RISE Together Mentorship Network for women of color in ministry, has been critical to the ongoing work of Union Theological Seminary in the City of New York, which makes space for this literary work possible.

Since 2017, the RISE Together Mentorship Network has established a multi-layered network of women of color mentors, mentee sojourners, theological institutions, and ecclesial partners across eight cities. For four years, Union Theological Seminary in the City of New York has provided the administrative and institutional anchor that has held space for the creation of a *Sacred Sistering* devotional by and for women of color. I would especially like to thank president Serene Jones who has always supported RISE and encouraged the publication of this important work. I am also grateful to academic dean, Pamela Cooper-White, faculty members Su Yon Pak, and Greg Snyder who were instrumental in promoting the value of RISE mentorship programming as a supplemental unit for student credit. Much appreciation is extended to various administrators and staff – Robin Reese, Ian Rees, Bethany Vaughn, Don Joshua, and Mike Malony for helping the RISE Mentorship Network build an administrative infrastructure that has helped to make space for documenting the voices and reflections of women ministry leaders of color.

Throughout this unprecedented year of pandemic, protests, and politics, I have been blessed to be surrounded by a sustaining sisterhood of women whose sistering presence, meticulous detail, gentle reminders, and follow-up have supported my efforts to bring the vision for a deeply meaningful and unique devotional to completion. *This Sacred Sistering: A Devotional for Wnistry* would not have come to fruition without the loving, affirming, and collective leadership of five phenomenal women of God, known as RISE's Sacred Sistering Review Team: Brittini Palmer, Diana Bien-aime Garrett, Wanda Paulk Holder, Chante Barrett, and Genise Reid.

Each review team member embodied an extraordinary spirit of commitment and excellence as they sacrificed several hours each month for one year organizing the devotional's five sections, reading, reviewing, and meeting with section writers, and sharing their feedback and encouragement. A special thank you to Brittini Palmer, RISE communication coordinator, who served with me as co-director of this writing project and created a well-organized communication method guided by the wisdom of a quarterly publication timeline created by Diana Bien-Aime Garrett, RISE communication volunteer. Wanda Paulk Holder, Atlanta-based RISE mentor, spent countless hours assisting me and Brittini in organizing biblical texts and section themes for dissemination and selection by interested contributors. Chante Barrett, RISE sojourner, class of 2020, and Genise Reid, RISE Part-Time Program Manager, provided valuable biblical reflections and critical feedback as the review team endeavored to reverence and celebrate the uniqueness of each literary voice. I celebrate and thank each of the review team members for joining me on this remarkable and unforgettable journey.

Words cannot express my gratitude for Taneki Dacres, Chief Executive Officer of Vine Publishing. Conversations with Taneki have been filled with the fruits of her experience and passion for ministry and publishing. She has pushed me every step of the way to ensure excellence in the final literary product. Thank you for such willingness to take this journey with RISE and to share your invaluable insight during every phase of this literary process.

Alisha Tatem, creator of the cover design and artwork is held with great admiration. Her imagination, creativity, patience, and ongoing support of me and the work of **RISE** have helped to bring the joy and thriving of women of color in ministry to life. Thank you for your artistic radiance.

Finally, with much gratitude and deep appreciation, I thank God for the work, wisdom, and wonder of all **RISE** women, mentors and mentee sojourners, the Class of 2020 and 2022. It has been inspiring to journey with such powerful women in eight cities across the country. A special thank you and acknowledgment to all the women who have contributed to the *Sacred Sistering* devotional. Your heart-felt prayers and words of reflection offer great inspiration and hope to women of color in ministry.

~Reverend Dr. Lisa Rhodes,
Executive Director of RISE

TABLE OF CONTENTS

INTRODUCTION

*D*uring my formative years, I was nurtured by the wisdom and resilience of women village keepers, communal and family rituals, and friends of distinction—my peer group of seven black ambitious and audacious teen girls, who Alice Walker would characterize as "wanting to be, and trying to be grown, yet girlish." In these sacred spaces and relationships, through the wisdom of elders, sistering friendships, prayer, and the breaking of bread, I experienced a relational God working through a spiritual mosaic of women in Christian community. My coming-of-age years within the context of a strong and affirming women-centered community, mirrored for me what being "My Sister's Keeper" and Sacred Sistering should mean and look like.

Sunday dinner around grandma's kitchen table and playing "double dutch" in the inner-city community of Brooklyn, New York, provided examples of an enduring commitment to relational and communal values of *Sistering* that has for 30 years influenced my ministry, and the creation of women-centered spaces. From "women at the well" Bible studies at Ebenezer Baptist Church in

Atlanta, Georgia and Payne Theological Seminary in Wilberforce, Ohio, to founding the Women in Spiritual Discernment of Ministry (WISDOM) Center at Spelman College, and RISE Together Mentorship Network for Women of Color in Ministry, anchored at Union Theological Seminary, I have learned the importance of holding safe and sacred space for women of faith to care for one another and counter oppressive forces through what I describe as *Sacred Sistering*.

Sacred Sistering is a practice of care, concern, and counsel shared between women of color through acts of love, kindness, counsel, laughter, dance, song, truth-telling, story-telling, and rituals. Sacred Sistering calls us to see our sisters, as reflections of the "Imago Dei;" and to dwell with each other in authenticity and vulnerability, the unknown and familiar, and in the comfortable and uncomfortable spaces of life. *Sacred Sistering* calls forth what is "most holy within ourselves and each other," and within that sacred space, reflect back to one another the presence, compassion, and love of God.

Sacred Sistering is designed as a collection of devotions, poems, and prayers to inspire women of color toward an enduring sense of faith, hope, and spiritual direction in life and ministry leadership. The uniqueness of this devotional is found when women of color reflect on the narratives of biblical women, their relationships with each other, and the issues that regulate women to the margins of culture, church, and community. The power lies in how women of color at the intersection of race, gender, and everyday life, find in the biblical narratives their own stories, untold truths, strength, hope, distress, disappointment, comfort, and practices of *Sacred Sistering* that empower and sustain them.

This dynamic devotional tells the varied truths and complexity of *Sacred Sistering* through the eyes and experiences of women in the RISE Together Mentorship Network. Devotions and prayers consist of hopeful and inspiring testimonies reflecting women's experiences, *Sistering* moments, and missed opportunities. *Sistering* moments that have assisted women through difficult transitions, relationships, and growing pains. Seasons in which joys, blessings, and accomplishments have been celebrated, and loneliness, invisibility, and the wounds of disempowerment have been comforted. Times when we have neglected, ignored, exploited or oppressed a sister, and asked for forgiveness and a second chance. Within the sacred spaces of this devotional, women of color in ministry and leadership explore the quality of sistering relationships, challenge conventional interpretations of biblical texts, and encourage faithful leadership. Through reflective devotions and prayers, we highlight racial and gender injustices and call forth deeper connections between women of color ministry leaders, and stronger support for their well-being.

Sacred Sistering: A Devotional for Women of Color in Ministry is divided into five sections: From Sisterhood to Sistering; Shades of Sistering; Seasons of Sistering; Generational Sistering; and Prayers for our Sisters, with a closing Epilogue, I RISE. Intended to **R**enew, **I**nspire, **S**upport, and **E**mpower the souls of women in ministry, Sacred Sistering devotions are for all who care about the ministry, leadership, spiritual life journey, and legacy of women of color. The following devotion and prayer sections are guided by the Spirit, and reflects the passion, activism, and multi-dimensional experiences of women of color.

~Reverend Dr. Lisa Rhodes,
Executive Director of RISE

FROM SISTERHOOD TO SISTERING

*T*his section lifts up heart-felt devotions that explore the joys of sistering moments, regrets, and missed opportunities, as well as experiences of tensed and challenging seasons that impact a woman's decision to support or abandon a sister. Sisterhood consists of both dyads and communal networks of women connected by a common interest, religion, vocation, and need. In times of hardship, joy, and pain, celebration, challenge, and achievements, sisterhood networks have historically served as a relational and organizational covering, conduit, and context for learning the practice of *Sacred Sistering* — a more intimate and interpersonal act of care, concern, and counsel given to women individually or collectively. Sisterhood provides the communal and collective mirror for the practice of *Sacred Sistering* that calls for a deeper interpersonal communion between each other and God. Moving from belonging to a sisterhood to embracing *Sacred Sistering* is a holy practice that calls each of us to a higher level of ethical responsibility for the care and support of our sisters of color in ministry and leadership.

REVEREND ANDREA D. LEWIS, PH.D.

The Ties That Bind — Ruth Clung to Naomi

"…your people shall be my people, and your God my God." (Ruth 1:16)

Ruth and Naomi's relationship is a beautiful model of the sisterhood among women in Christ. Family circumstances of loss, sadness, and survival brought them together, *but* their love for each other, expressed in their sistering and mothering relationships, sustained their journey. Many of us as children, teenagers and young adults have experienced this type of sistering and mothering in relationships with older women.

I was blessed to have a Naomi and Ruth type of love in my life with Aunt Lou, my adoptive grandmother who guided me through the seasons of infanthood, childhood, adolescence, and young womanhood. She planted the seeds of knowledge and kept me in line through the seasons.

Because Aunt Lou had no children of her own, her neighbors, friends, and family members knew and loved me. I attended family reunions and to this day, her family continues to welcome me with open arms. Just like Ruth and Naomi, they were my people. The bonds transcended blood lines and were empowered by God's love.

Just as Naomi nurtured Ruth, Aunt Lou provided loving support over the years. Even after her death, I hear her words of wisdom that guide me through the highs and lows. Ruth and Naomi had a one-of-a-kind relationship. They were more than daughter-in-law and mother-in-law. They were sistered. Their relationship encompassed the joys and pains through the seasons of life we as ministerial leaders face daily. After the deaths of their husbands, Ruth clung to Naomi, learning lessons and growing in God just as we nurture the relationships in our congregations, and with sisters and mothers in ministry.

Who are those kind-hearted women in your life who encouraged you to live by God's principles, offered countless words of advice, and tough love? They are sisters and mothers, women with gracious spirits, confident strides, and a love for God that permeates their souls. Who represents Naomi and Ruth in your life? As you journey through your calling, ground your relationships with sistering and mothering, in sacred love, through unyielding acceptance, and by graceful longevity.

PRAYER: *Dear God, we thank you for sending women in our lives to grow with us, celebrate with us, cry with us, and walk with us through the seasons. Help us to love each other with steadfast loyalty like Ruth and Naomi, sisters and mother-like figures bound in your sweet love. Amen.*

 **Reverend Andrea Dais Lewis, Ph.D.** is an ordained Itinerant Deacon, Associate Minister at Big Bethel African Methodist Episcopal Church in Atlanta, and founder of Virtuous Pearl Interdenominational Women's Ministry.

REVEREND BRITTINI L. PALMER

We are Sisters, not the Oppressor: Resist Sexism

"…go in to my maid; it may be that I shall obtain children by her."

(Genesis 16:2)

*W*e know what oppression feels like. We know what it's like for someone to ignore our greatness, take our ideas, and underpay us. We also know the feeling of having the power to make decisions that affect our sisters. We are often the oppressed, and if we're honest, we are also like our oppressors. Sometimes, we use and manipulate each other when it benefits us. One day we're Sarai and the next Hagar. We impregnate other women with our mess, and when they experience complications, we leave them, and that's not sistering.

Truthfully, we are often placed in complex positions. When we encounter each other, our wires have intentionally been crossed. Our *communication, compassion, counsel, and care* are tied up in violent systems. Maybe this was the start of Hagar and Sarai's relationship. Perhaps, their wires were crossed before they said one word to each other. They lived as though their value was measured by who could follow societal rules the best. They were women in a system that measured their worth by how much the man is pleased with them and whether they produce requisite babies. We, like them, may never have experienced the authenticity of sacred sistering. They experienced false realities and man-made ideas, and yet, throughout it all, God still desired to make broken things whole again.

God in his majestic way is ever present when dealing with the pains of the world, and yet repeatedly we miss divine moments to sister each other. We exist in systems and miss God. We can operate with our eyes closed, bodies tensed, and minds cluttered just like Sarai and Hagar. They were connected by the institutions of slavery and marriage in a patriarchal world. They were bonded under clouds filled with injustice. These conditions for anyone can create insecurities, making us believe a problem is fixed, but all we did was transfer the pain.

I am guilty of this. I've gotten caught up in circles of violence. I've believed what society said I should be and therefore hurt other Black women. I have. I didn't know who I was and didn't care about the sister I mistreated for societal accolades. As I reflect, I can clearly see how we lead our sisters into dark places, refusing to show them the way out. We have the power to navigate this world differently. From my mother, to my sisters, friends, and strangers, I first see them. We are sisters not our oppressors, and if we want to live, we must never forget that.

So, before we try to be the best in the room, let us breathe, and look around. This one breath can be the difference between sisterhood and sistering. This moment allows us to remember who we are, see, and connect. We have the ability to do this. We must. Because evil is ever present, the world needs us, and most importantly, we need each other.

PRAYER: *God. Help us not to become what we fight against. Amen.*

Reverend Brittini L. Palmer is a freedom writer, public theologian, and Communications Consultant, who currently resides in Atlanta, Georgia. Visit her blog - https://www.brittinilpalmer.com/blog

REVEREND TIFFANY BURCH

Why We Push Our Sisters Away

"...Turn back, my daughters, why will you go with me?" (Ruth 1:11)

"Why do we do what we do?" A simple, but meaningful question I've often heard growing up. Asking "why," causes us to reflect, unveil masked emotions, approach hidden truths, and possibly discern answers. Asking "why" is important because it helps us unlearn behaviors and identify patterns and doctrines we've embraced over time. When we expose our hidden truths, we get to the root of our "why?" Naomi advised her daughters-in-law to leave her at a time when she probably needed them the most. Why would she do that? Why do many of us push away people willing to be there for us, and why don't we speak up when we are in need? Perhaps Naomi felt she would be a burden to her daughters-in-law, or she felt she had nothing to offer. Perhaps you've pushed your sisters away because you've felt like you have nothing to offer—you feel as if your life experiences, gifts, and talents are of no value.

The reality is, in our attempt to avoid grappling with our self-worth, we push our sisters away and neglect moments of growth. Naomi questioned why Ruth and Orpah would want to stay in connection with her because she had nothing to contribute to their growth. Instead of viewing her circumstances as a pathway to inspire, encourage, and impart on her daughters-in-law, Naomi used it as an excuse to push them away. Naomi centered her relationship on what she could offer, rather than on what could be gained.

Many of us, like Naomi, force our sisters away because we think no one understands or that we can bear our burdens without the help of our sisters. It was not about perseverance, but about overcoming insecurities and pride so God's gift of community could be embraced. Perhaps Naomi felt the need to be alone in her suffering so Ruth and Orpah wouldn't suffer with her. Naomi's personal experience of pain and being overlooked appears in her attempt to exile Ruth and Orpah. How has women of color in ministry been overlooked and how has that experience shaped how they view their sisters?

Maybe you have been a part of spaces and ministries in which you were unnoticed, worked with individuals that didn't see your worth or made you doubt your gifts and talents. Sometimes, feelings of doubt, low-self-esteem, rejection, and not being good enough can build up and cause you to detach from your sisters and the promises God has declared over your life. How are you addressing those emotions that rise up and try to prevent you from receiving the love of your sisters? Have you asked yourself what is associated with those fears and emotions? Sis, you must get to the root of your why so that the way you view yourself and your sisters can be restored and changed. It is not God's intention for God's daughters to sojourn alone. God sends you sisters that will not only embrace you, but also journey with you. Sisters that will encourage you to embrace yourself. Don't let self-doubt be projected on those embracing you. Position yourself to receive your sisters (Ruths) and know your worth. So, Sister, I charge you to rise up and know that you are not alone!

PRAYER: *God, help me to embrace my sisters with love and help me to know that I am not alone on this journey. Amen.*

Reverend Tiffany Burch provides leadership, care, and guidance to children and youth, using innovative methods to dismantle false doctrines.

MONICA LEAK

Do This, Not That: Becoming a Better Sister

"...and when she saw that she had conceived, she looked on me with contempt." (Genesis 16:5)

*A*s the oldest sibling, I was held accountable for everything my younger sister said and did. I felt like I got in trouble for her stuff. It did not help matters that if I wanted to go anywhere, it was an automatic "take your sister with you," requirement. Being a teenager, I was focused on developing my own identity and forging friendships/relationships with no consideration for my younger sibling who was now faced with the same struggles I faced as a daughter of ministers. I missed some opportunities to sister in a way that would have given her some insight and strategies. Looking back I can now see where I could have been a better listener, a more attentive and understanding sister. As women in color in ministry, moving from sisterhood to sistering requires discovering ways to be better listeners, more attentive, and understanding of each other.

We can look at the story of Hagar and Sarai for some do's and don'ts on moving from sisterhood to sistering.

Hagar was a servant in the house of Abraham and she was subject to the rules of the house. While she may or may not have been excited about becoming a conduit for Sarai to have a child, she discovered the joy. We learn from Hagar that, when you become pregnant with purpose, a dream, or a vision, you rejoice.

Do this: *Rejoice in the Lord always; again, I will say, Rejoice* (Philippians 4:4). Whether you liked the circumstance that brought you into the birthing position or not, you are now responsible for bringing forth what God has placed inside you. So, girl, "Birth it!" Birth the book, write, edit, publish, and repeat! Birth that music, sing, record, copyright your work, and repeat. Get those sermons out of your back pocket and go live.

Not that: *Become prideful and engaging with others with an air of superiority over an accomplishment.* "...And when she saw that she had conceived, she looked with contempt on her mistress," (Genesis 16:4b). For Hagar, this was an opportunity for her to embrace her mistress Sarai as her servant instead of antagonizing her, which caused a shift in the environment. As women in ministry, we can acknowledge the gifts that we bring to the table and do so in love and humility. Our work and effort will speak for themselves.

Do this: *Acknowledge your role and seek forgiveness* (Psalms 51:3, James 5:16). In Genesis 16:5, Sarai lashes out at Abram for Hagar's contempt of her after conception. We do not see Sarai acknowledge her role as the initiator of Hagar and Abram's union. Like Sarai, as women in ministry you will come across some situations in which you are not always in the right. Acknowledge the mistake, make the effort to correct so that healing can take place, and you become better and not bitter in your sistering.

Not That: *Allow the roots of jealousy, envy or pride to hinder you from moving in what God has promised you.* From the text (Genesis 16:1-3), you can see how jealousy impacted a relationship. As women in ministry, we can find ourselves caught in a comparison trap and caught in our feelings when things don't happen our way. If you become stuck in the place of jealousy, envy, or pride, how can you move into that which God has promised you?

Do this: *Identify the problem and have the conversation to bring healing and understanding.* While the text does not tell us whether Sarai or Hagar had a heart-to-heart conversation upon her return to the household, we do know that the seed of both Sarai and Hagar would become nations. We are reminded in Matthew 18:15 how to have those conversations. As women in ministry, there will be those conversations that are easily had and those which we dread, but to bring about the healing and understanding, we must be willing to make that stretch.

Your situation may not be easily resolved, but make the initial effort and leave the rest to God. Today, Hagar and Sarai's problem would be considered a hot mess, but you have the opportunity to do this and not that to become a better sister.

PRAYER: *Lord, today, help me to rejoice, show up in love, and do my work, so I can be a better sister. Amen.*

 Speech-language pathologist, academic librarian, poet and associate minister, **Monica Leak** uses the power of words to share the gospel through creative content.

Why Are You Distracted? Don't Blame Your Sister

"Martha was distracted with much serving…'Lord, do you not care that my sister has left me to serve alone?'" (Luke 10:40)

I wonder if you are like me, an ambitious woman of God. You've got your time schedule down to the last second of the day. Meetings, classes, bible study, preaching, teaching, counseling…always moving, serving, and giving. Like Martha, you have things to do, people to see, and places to go. You are a busy woman. Can you relate? Sis, I can relate. But here's the thing. Sometimes God is just waiting for us to PAUSE, pray, listen, and obey. The text tells us that Martha was busy and distracted by serving, but Mary sat at the feet of Jesus. I can only imagine that Mary was experiencing peace, joy, and comfort in the presence of Jesus. Mary had one priority sitting and listening to Jesus. She chose to be present and soak in his presence rather than to be at work. Mary wanted to take it ALL in. She was ready to receive and be filled. She allowed herself the time to breathe, and more importantly, she permitted herself to receive.

Like Martha, you have found yourself in a similar situation, trying to figure how to get it all done—for example, sermon writing, ministering to those experiencing poverty, praying for the sick, and taking care of your family. One might imagine Martha thinking, "Now I am supposed to host a party for our visitors? My sister is supposed to help me, yet there she is, sitting and basking in the presence of our honorable guest." Who would not be emotional? It doesn't help that the Holy man says, "sister, sit, you are worried and distracted by many things." Your distress is obvious. You are probably thinking but not saying, "Can't you see what's going on here? Why did you not send someone over to help me? I asked her for help, and she ignored me. I am stunned that you think my working was wrong and that her sitting and relaxing was a better choice? I do not understand. I feel dismissed, hurt, and aggravated!"

If you have experienced similar feelings, let us fight against the oppression that deceives us, compelling us to believe we must work by ourselves and not find time to rest. As women of color and women in ministry, we must remember the presence and anointing of God are available to us by God's grace. Our sister-friends can assist in difficult times and are here to help and not hurt. You are not expected to do it all by yourself. You are not alone. Ask, and it will be given to you.

Sis, you have been juggling family, life, and ministry for a long time, and now you are overwhelmed. You have been giving and giving of yourself, and now you're feeling depleted. Sis, it's time to rest.

PRAYER: *Lord, help me to be still, to remain in your presence, to trust you with all things, and to make the better choices all the days of my life.*

 Minister Elaine Robinson Beattie, *RCC, MSML, MRL,* Inspirational Speaker, Leadership Coach, and Trainer Inspiring Inclusive Leadership, Atlanta, GA.

ELDER DR. TIFFANY STUBBS

A Blessing for My Sister

"And Mary remained with her…" (Luke 1:56)

My earliest memories of sisterhood occurred much like this biblical narrative of Elizabeth and Mary: intergenerational sharing of ideas, concerns, and what they carried. I vividly remember seeing how sisterhood involves the intentional duality of both *being and doing*. Being and doing encompassed what I remember my grandmother and her friends summarized in these wisdom nuggets: *Sisters speak life to each other, sisters BE there for each other, and sisters always provide space to grow.* This is what I believe sistering looks like. It's not just a title, or shared blood lineage, but it's the active participation of sisters, sharing the weight of what God has placed inside of them. It's the beauty of Elizabeth and Mary as they commemorate their birthing experience with blessing each other.

The blessing isn't contingent on how long they haven't seen each other, or even the length of distance. This blessing proclaimed by both was the affirmation of what they knew to be true: they shared a bond. A bond that even difference in age or social location could not disintegrate. A bond that the seeds of hope they both carried communicated with each other metaphysically. Now, I could imagine that Elizabeth probably had a few questions about Mary's pregnancy. However, the glorious thing revealed in the text is that Elizabeth admonished Mary by reminding her of the favor that was upon her. She maximized the divine moment by being open to the Spirit and sharing life-giving words. As women of color in ministry, our bonds of sistering are strengthened and illuminated as we remain open to the divine Spirit. This openness pivots us into Spirit-filled exchanges that are conduits for encouragement, hope, and love.

I recall the moments on my grandmother's front porch when I first saw the practice of sisterhood to sistering. I lived for the summer days when I could have a seat and listen to their testimonies. I long for the days of seeing them interact as they prepare gingerbread. I reminisce on the times when I would hear the knock on the door and they would ask each other to borrow a cup of sugar. The sharing of sugar was a rite of passage for their sistering. Sharing sweetness and holding space for the bittersweet, were the fabrics of their sistering tapestry.

Sistering is the remembering of testimonies, the recommencing of triumphs, and the re-aligning of purpose…together. Mary shared a song, after Elizabeth blessed her. What songs of blessings and gratitude do you have for your sisters? I pray the sweet memories of sistering blessings flow into beautiful composition of songs that last a lifetime.

PRAYER: *May you experience sistering at its purest and laugh without hesitation as the cords of sisterhood grow stronger, as you bless one another. Amen.*

Elder Dr. Tiffany Stubbs is an ordained elder and licensed Pharmacist in Birmingham, Al.

Sistering Moments

" 'For with God nothing will be impossible…' Mary arose and went with haste into the hill country, to a city of Judah." (Luke 1: 37, 39)

I grew up with two older brothers who did not want their little sister tagging along with them. I longed to have a sister I could play dress up and dolls with. Someone I could tell all my secrets to and know they would not leave the safety of our relationship. Someone who would know me deeply and not judge me. I longed for this. And I'm grateful that over the years, God gifted me with women who truly "sistered" me. They helped me to manifest the divine purpose for my life even when I did not always understand it and it seemed impossible.

I can imagine Mary longed for this kind of sisterly relationship after she received news she would become the mother of Christ. "How could this be?", was her initial response. This news would turn her world upside down and could have cost her reputation, marriage, and possibly her life. She needed someone to share this secret with, and it had to be someone that would not judge her, doubt her, or think she was crazy for believing what seemed impossible. Who could she share this with? Her mother? Her father?

The narrative never mentions where Mary's mother or father was during this troubling and confusing time. But Luke records that, instead of Mary confiding in her parents or even her fiancé, she runs to Elizabeth's house in Judea who was experiencing a miracle of her own.

The fact that Mary visits Elizabeth after she receives this news, suggests there are some situations we go through in life where WE must connect with sisters who understand that God works best in what seems impossible. A sister whose "miracle" leaps inside of her when we come into her presence. A sister who realizes the miracle and destiny God is birthing in us is divinely connected to what God is birthing in her. Elizabeth and Mary's relationship reveal that a part of sacred sistering is being able to imagine the impossible for one another.

As women in ministry may we hold onto the example Elizabeth and Mary set before us to "sister" each other into our collective destinies.

·

PRAYER: *Creator God, thank you for sistering moments. May we understand the power sistering has in helping us manifest the divine purpose and calling on our lives. Amen.*

 **Reverend Dr. Alisha Tatem** is a minister, artist, counselor, preacher, and community leader who is passionate about building bridges across diverse communities and helping individuals fulfill their purpose and live into their destiny.

MINISTER DEIRDRE JONESE AUSTIN

I Need to Spend Time With My Sisters

"Let this thing be done for me…" (Judges 11:37)

"Grant me two months, so that I may go and wander on the mountains, and bewail my virginity, my companions and I" (Judges 11: 36). This is the one request Jephthah's daughter makes of her father upon his return from battle. Sometimes the decisions of others lead us to situations in which we need sistering. It is with our sisters that we can find a space to be and stand in our truth.

While Jephthah's daughter may have seemed calm, composed, and understanding in the interaction with her father, I imagine her conversation with her sisters went a little differently. It was with them that she could be her full self and express all her emotions around the news that she was to be sacrificed.

"How could he make such a vow? How could God allow this to happen? I've been nothing but faithful. I don't deserve this. My dream of starting my own family and of raising children is gone. Why, God, Why?"

I imagine that her sisters listened. They affirmed her in her bewailing. They provided a space for her to be. To cry. To grieve. To break down. To remember. To mourn dreams that will never be realized. Together they lamented, but they also praised God for the moments they had together. They celebrated the time shared. They had fun, and they found joy amid the difficult circumstances.

Now, we all have moments where we may feel like Jephthah's daughter. Life was going well until "it" happened. That moment we got news that turned our lives upside down. News that shook us to our core. News that left us wondering, "Why, God, why?"

For me, that moment was when my father passed away unexpectedly over winter break leading into my junior year. I had prayed and had all faith that God would heal him, but it didn't happen. I couldn't focus on that because I had to get back to school. The semester was starting, and I had people on campus depending on me. I acted like everything was okay. Yet, I had some sisters who listened, affirmed, and provided a space for me to be. To cry. To grieve. To break down. To remember. I had some sisters who provided space for me to lament as well as experience moments of fun and joy. To laugh in the midst of my pain. I am thankful that, like Jephthah's daughter, I have some sisters. May this scripture be a reminder that amid difficulties, we can lean into our community, and count on our sisters.

PRAYER: *God, thank you for giving me sisters who can provide me with the space and support I need as I experience the joys and trials of life's journey. Amen.*

Minister Deirdre "Jonese" Austin is a minister, writer, and justice seeker in the Candler Atlanta RISE cohort who is committed to employing a radical love ethic in working towards healing, wholeness, and liberation through good theology, research, direct action, and policy.

SHADES OF SISTERING

*T*his section highlights a variety of textures, trials, and triumphs sisters experience between and with each other. How women of color in ministry and leadership show up for each other, stand in solidarity, honor, support, respect, affirm difference and freedom of choice, without dismissing or "Othering," are central to *Sacred Sistering* Through   s h a d e s and varieties of interpersonal   a n d relational experiences, sistering occasionally mirrors internalized oppressive cultural values that can adversely influence the choices women make in their female relationships. Shades of *Sistering* signify the degree of light and darkness a sister gives or is exposed to by another sister. The level and quality of commitment and care a sister is willing to offer in order to prevent and protect another sister from harmful exposure that injures her well-being, exists on a continuum of low to high. How women of color encourage, edify, and enhance the light and Holy within a sister aligns with the high end of the *Sacred Sistering* continuum.

REVEREND AUDREY WILLIAMSON

Female Bonding-Female Relationship:

The Sacred Spirit of Sisterhood

"So she set out from the place where she was, with her two daughters-in-law..." (Ruth 1:7)

*I*n the ancient text, we read of the relationship between Orpah, Ruth, and Naomi. A relationship between a mother-in-law and a daughter-in-law can be simultaneously problematic, tension-filled, ambivalent, or even adversarial. If we are honest, the truth of the matter is women, no matter their occupation, age or marital status can sometimes mirror some of these attributes.

As a woman who has seen friendships come and go, some through neglect, others by way of betrayal, some as a result of distance and ambivalence, I can confirm that maintaining relationships, remaining bonded and connected, can be a challenge. Life gets busy, our bonds may be primarily work or family related, and the strength of these friendships may be malleable and easily abandoned in the "busyness" of life.

Recently, I traveled to California to visit with my godfather, who had lost his wife several years ago. They were my second parents, in every way one can imagine. Their daughter, 5 years younger than I, are close and bonded as true sisters. We do not speak often. She has yet to marry and has no children; my marriage is mature, and I am now experiencing the joy of being a grandmother. She pursued her business degree, and has little interest in organized religion; I preach and teach faith for a living. Our lives are, in many ways, diametrically opposite. Yet, whenever we get together, it is as though no time has passed; we are able to pick up where we last ended.

Through the ancient text, through our own experiences, we are reminded that every relationship has an expiration date: some relationships are for a reason, others for a season, and still others for a lifetime. All serve a purpose, and we are wise to evaluate the purpose and productivity of all of our connections. The deep friendship of Ruth and Naomi is an example of support and general respect between women. The two were of a different faith, born of different generations, and, after the death of their husbands, had no real abiding connection. It was a relationship we should model; a relationship among "sisters" that nourishes and sustains, through difficulties, loss, grief, joys and triumphs, as well as the everyday mundanities of life.

It is my hope that we will find at least one sister to share this deep and abiding bond, despite time and distance, changes and challenges. I am grateful that I have a bond with my "sister", one that has endured for more than 50 years!

PRAYER: *Lord, help us to be true friends to our sisters. Give us the insight to follow our own heart as we serve you. Amen.*

Audrey Akins Williamson is an ordained Elder in the AME Zion Church, serving as Associate Minister at the historic Mother Zion Church in Harlem. She is also the Director of the Collaborative for

TONYA JOHNSON

Before I Let Go

"But Ruth said, 'Entreat me not to leave you or to return from following you; for where you go I will go, and where you lodge I will lodge...' " (Ruth 1:16)

Frankie Beverly and Maze, and later Beyonce, had a popular hit song entitled, "Before I Let Go." In both versions, Frankie Beverly and Beyonce thanked God that the sun rises and shines on the other person. I love this song for multiple reasons. First, I can't help but move and groove to the beat, but second, the lyrics, which says, "You stood right beside me...and I won't forget", is a reminder for me of the importance of sisterhood and the need for sistering. We need each other to survive the trials of ministry. Shades of sistering means standing in solidarity with each other, thanking God for each other, and committing to supporting one another.

When life got rough, and the future was uncertain, Ruth held on to Naomi. Who are you holding onto or who's holding onto you? Ruth would not abandon Naomi, and as sisters of color in ministry, we too must not abandon each other.

There have been many times in my life when I have been

encouraged, and then there were times when I have had to encourage others. There were times when I wanted to let go of all the demands of family, school and ministry, but then a sister was there to uplift me. There are times when you may want to let go; times when life gets overwhelming; times when it's all too much to handle, but before you let go, know that your sisters are there with you. We need each other during times of trials and tribulations.

Before you let go, a true sister-friend will provide comforting words and even assistance to help you make it through a tough time. During challenging moments, a ride-or-die sister will be there to take you to that medical appointment, be the shoulder to cry on, babysit your kids, or just be there with a listening ear. Before you let go, or before she lets go, call, text, and be there.

Sis, I thank God for you. I thank God for your sacrifice. I thank God for your ministry. Like the song says, thank God that the sun rises and shines on you. Life and ministry will not always be easy, but in the words of Ruth, where you go, your sisters will go, and where you lodge, your sisters will lodge. No matter what comes our way, let us continue to uplift and uphold each other.

Sis, don't let go.

PRAYER: *God, even when we feel like letting go, help us to hold on. Give us the strength to keep pressing forward. Give us the courage to uphold our sisters. Lord, help us not to let go. Amen.*

Tonya Johnson, class valedictorian, graduated with a Master of Divinity degree from the Samuel DeWitt Proctor School of Theology at Virginia Union University in

Ending a Friendship: Taking a Different Path

"Orpah kissed her mother-in-law, but Ruth clung to her." (Ruth 1:14)

*H*ave you endured a relationship that you knew would demand more than it would give, but you stayed anyway? Orpah's voluntary departure opened a pathway for us to follow because she walked toward the hope of being defined not by loss, but instead by what could be gained. We all deserve to walk toward that, as luxury that should reflect our reality—a belief and hope in what awaits us that is not yet seen.

Despite thousands of years between our present moment and that of Naomi, Ruth and Orpah, today, as women in ministry who offer pastoral care and leadership, embody intersectionality, and fulfill multiple roles in our families and society, our lives are still too often defined by our relationships with others: those in the past or at present, those we have lost, those with a cost.

Why didn't or haven't you let go? What influenced your assessment that the cost of holding on was one you could absorb?

These three biblical women share a bond deepened through grief and trauma. Naomi laments as a mother. All three women grieve as widows. Although thousands of years ago, their trifecta of tragic loss seems not so distant to us 21st century women who far too frequently lose our kin to preventable causes: sickness reflecting systemic neglect; lethal compound violence targeting Black, Brown and LGBTQ+ bodies—from sources they tell us we should trust.

Ruth responded to Naomi's unspoken fear of being left alone. Sometimes we need sisters like that, who see what we need and spring into action despite the words we exclaim. And we also need sisters like Orpah, who honored Naomi's verbal expressions. Orpah represents our sisters who hold us accountable for declaring what we want and need in a world that has silenced us, forced stereotypical perceptions upon us, and diminished our worth.

Beloved, declaring your needs and wants rejects the expectation to conform and leads to actions that reflect who we know ourselves to be in God's eyes. Let us honor our gift of life and salvation by honoring our ability to choose in a world that tries so hard to limit our existence.

PRAYER: *Help us God, to use our words and actions to be a blessing to others and to ourselves by declaring, and claiming, our authentic needs and wants in all our relationships.* Asé. Awoman. Let it be so.

Minister Kimberley Gordy is an M.Div. student at Union Theological Seminary in the City of New York, and has been located

REVEREND CARLA JEAN-MCNEIL JACKSON, ESQUIRE

Beyond Bitterness and Depression

"And she replied, 'All that you say I will do.' " (Ruth 3:5)

The Naomi-Ruth story starts in distress. Famine forced Naomi's family to move. Then Naomi's husband and sons died, leaving Naomi and the local women her sons married, Ruth and Orpah, widowed and without status. Having no male sponsor, they had to survive in a time when women were powerless and without assurance of safety. It is no wonder that Naomi's first phrases are lyrics of lament and declarations of distancing (see Ruth 1:12-13).

She lamented...we lament. The reality is, we have that same tendency to give up during hard times. We abandon others and ourselves because we do not believe we can triumph over tragedy. And who can blame us when our reality, especially as women leaders of color, is often one of closed doors, damaging stereotypes, or stolen ideas?

Having been the first and only woman of color executive in a workplace at one time, I identify with this isolating experience. I know what it's like having few resources and little support, being looked over and left out, remaining silent about mistreatment, or being labeled as a complainer or difficult. I know what it's like to see the sovereign God as the ultimate source, while like Naomi, feel like "the Almighty has dealt bitterly" with me (Ruth 1:20). So that bitterness and depression do not control us, we need a plan to cope with calamity.

Naomi and Ruth championed the ethic of Sistering—by standing in solidarity to resist ruin. I commend this code of conduct to all women of color leaders who experience trauma and isolation. Misery could have paralyzed Naomi, causing her to quit believing she could not manage misfortune. Yet, she persisted, with Ruth's nudging, and they provide a parable of what is possible when marginalized women work together and employ our ingenuity. By working together, they survived.

Similarly, we can weather catastrophic circumstances through Sistering. To embody this ethic, we, first, cultivate community. Meaning, we build a network of care by connecting with others, because together we win. I united with similar leaders to share experiences and extend support through the storms. When Naomi tried to isolate herself, Ruth refused, and they negotiated the new normal together, which restored Naomi's hope for living. That anticipation activated her agency, the final ethic of Sistering. Here, like Alice Walker, we love ourselves 'regardless'— unashamedly taking matters into our own hands to prosper and not perish.

While some may critique choices made in mayhem, Naomi strategized for survival—unapologetically utilizing Ruth's resources. And Ruth "went down to the threshing floor and did just as [Naomi] had instructed her" (Ruth 3:6). Later, the story shows Naomi and Ruth's significance extending beyond their lifetimes, so failing to unify in turmoil would have disrupted their legacy and stifled the very breath of God.

Therefore, let us personify the Sistering principle by cultivating our community and activating our agency, so that we can move beyond despair to thrive in threatening times.

PRAYER: *Empower us, Lord, to love ourselves and our sisters through struggle; and help us compassionately configure new ways of being because our heritage hinges on the here and now. Amen.*

The Reverend Carla Jean-McNeil Jackson, Esquire is a licensed attorney, ordained minister, and proud member of Delta Sigma Theta Sorority, Incorporated.

REVEREND. DR. CLARENCIA SHADE

The Midwife Leads the Revolution--Save The Children

"When you serve as midwife to the Hebrew women, and see them upon the birthstool, if it is a son, you shall kill him; but if it is a daughter, she shall live." (Exodus 1:16).

hat do you do when your ministry calling directly opposes the law of the land? What is your weapon? Defying the system of slave masters is risky business. But, sometimes breaking the rules for the sake of justice is ordained by God.

The Midwives of Exodus defied the King's orders to kill male newborns. Fearful of being exposed and labeled as rebellious, they wrestled with their response. They grappled with discerning their ministry calling under an oppressive Egyptian system. They are conscientious objectors who understand that breaking the rules and not obeying the law of the land is unsafe. However, this midwife squad includes Mama Wisdom and they answer to a higher authority. They now embody the weapon of wisdom which enables them to operate undercover. Mama Wisdom is deployed and leads the way. Shipra, Puah, and Mama Wisdom appear on the scene completing the midwife squad.

Mama Wisdom counsels the midwives in secret and they weigh the case together. She brings clarity, courage, and the power necessary to save the children. She brings ancestral "mother-wit" and creativity, braided with Holy Spirit to win the revolution. The midwives are guided by their surrendered hearts while Wisdom sharpens their discernment to complete the will of God.

We, women of color ministry leaders are midwives faced with challenging decisions every day. The struggle is real. We must remember you are not alone. Mama Wisdom comes to assist you to lead a movement of liberation and not bondage, love not hate, peace not war; life and not death.

Let's close our eyes and listen for her words. Let Wisdom speak. Ask her to speak over us. Elevate your vantage point so we may focus on the bigger picture. Enlist warrior sisters to stand in the gap between this present age and future nations. We are the blood guardians of the innocent. We are leading the revolution of liberation, for saving our children is saving ourselves. Continue a fearless covert battle freeing those under your charge. Let us help each other birth creation placing God's fingerprint on the womb of every woman. Be bold in kingdom work, making no apologies. Mama Wisdom will empower us as we refuse to be intimidated by persons or systems threatening our future heritage…always leading by example.

PRAYER: *Lord, teach me the way of Wisdom as I strive to follow the path that leads to victory. Amen.*

Reverend Dr. Clarencia Shade, LCSW, M.d, TH.d CEO Gifts of Healing LLC/ Senior Elder Gifts of Healing Ministries.

REVEREND K. FARROW

Moving Beyond Competition and Flourishing
in Collaboration

" 'Behold, your maid is in your power; do to her as you please.' Then Sarai dealt harshly with her, and she fled from her." (Genesis 16:6)

*I*n relationship between Sarai and Hagar is one filled with contention and strife. It had all the crafting of sisterhood gone wrong. Sisterhood is power and a bond that can change the world and heal another person. It is sisterhood that gives strength to those who feel like there is no hope or support. It is sisterhood that helps us flourish as black women, and it is sisterhood that is the birthing place for all things beautiful, black, and brilliant. In the relationship between Sarai and Hagar, sisterhood turns sour, and once it does, trauma masking itself as a righteous option creates tribulation.

When Sarai became "convinced" she could not give her husband a child, she decided to intervene in a divine plan. By taking matters into her own hands, she initiated trauma by involving another woman to birth a child that was not a part of her destiny. Sarai's limited faith caused her to make a misguided decision that caused consequences for her and Hagar. Sis, has unbelief in God's promises caused you to make decisions contrary to your destiny, which brought trauma into your journey?

Hagar thought she was worth more than Sarai because she could bear children. The trauma of that wound created jealousy, envy, and even hatred. None of these intense emotions centers on sisterhood or community. Vulnerability, compassion, and connection need to be fostered in this relationship, not contempt and meanness. Sarai should have shown more mercy toward Hagar. Hagar could have softened her arrogance toward Sarai. This would have strengthened their bond, sisterhood would be glorified, and wholeheartedness toward one another would be their new path. Partnering with your sister leads to holistic healing that allows all to grow and flourish.

As we center sisterly affection, we must be careful not to hold space for strong negative emotions because they lead us toward poor decisions and harmful behaviors. Those behaviors do not center Christ as the love and light of our lives. If these sisters displayed a tender grace toward each other, it could have led them both from competition to collaboration. When we declare to our sister and show that we are interested in partnering with her, we'll see a relationship that flourishes and supports each other's destiny.

In the winter of our lives, let us try curating a community

of women who show up for each other in supportive and loving ways. Thus, when Spring comes, we'll see the blossoming buds of a relationship born from the love and admiration we have for our sister.

As Rise Sojourners, let us encourage each other to flourish and breathe in the freedom of collaborating with each other. Remember, the difference between a wound and a scar is, a scar is the evidence a wound has mended, and the trauma is gone. Sisters, let's center sisterhood as an antidote for healing trauma, not creating it.

PRAYER: *Gracious God, grant me the wisdom to be free and fearless. The clarity to make decisions from a heart and mind rooted in gratitude, love, and peace. Grant me the power to let go of scarcity and release decisions made from fear. In Black Jesus name, Amen.*

Reverend Dr. Kelly U. Farrow is the CEO, of The Kelly U. Farrow Institute for Black Preaching & Education & Creator & Principal, *Circle of SacredFire* ○ *Preaching Intensive for Women of Color in Ministry.*

REVEREND SYDNEY M. AVENT, ESQ.

I Refuse: Moving Beyond Oppression Toward Liberation

"…and she did not come…" (Esther 1:17)

N o.

A complete sentence

Emphatic

Freedom

Seemingly spare and sparse, but richly overflowing with promise and potential

Seemingly isolated and alone, but invisibly cocooned in sister spirits

Seemingly bland and colorless, but washed in the spiced tears of our foremothers

Our living, our being as proof that NO availeth much

Our NO as promise of plans to prosper us

Our NO as yes to God within, without, and around

Drawn from the well of the NO's of our sisters before us

Deposited into the sustaining waters for sisters walking with and behind us

Transmitted telepathically into perpetuity

NO, with love for ourself and our sisters!

As you imagine right actions today, allow yourself to tap into the spiritual ecosystem of our sisters; draw from the strength and wisdom others have deposited; and enrich the ecosystem by adding your light, strength, and wisdom.

PRAYER: *Creator and spirit God, you have made us uniquely one to thrive in community with many. We thank you for the sister ecosystem, which nurtures us, prods us, and supports us as we grow into our fully evolved personhood, more than we could have ever imagined or hoped.*

Rev. Sydney M. Avent, Esq. is a minister ordained in the Christian Church (Disciples of Christ) who serves God and God's people

REVEREND DR. IMANI-SHEILA NEWSOME-CAMARA

Remembering Queen Vashti : The Necessity of Knowing

"But Queen Vashti refused to come at the King's command…" (Esther 1:12)

*V*ashti was a daughter of Babylon's King and Queen. They, along with wise teachers, taught her to appreciate her gifts of wisdom and beauty. When family tragedy resulted in the death of her parents, Vashti had one option: to marry King Ahasuerus who made Vashti the Queen of Persia. King Ahasuerus focused on Vashti's beauty, demanding that she come to him naked adorned only in her royal crown. We are not privy to Queen Vashti's discernment process, yet we know she refused to obey his command. Rather than yield to public humiliation, she said, "NO," enraging King Ahasuerus to the point where "anger burned within him". Vashti's "NO" prompted King Ahasuerus to force her into exile. Yet Queen Vashti's NO—rooted in the knowledge of her worth and dignity—gave her the ability to reject oppression and choose self-respect.

My father, mother and family taught me to value my wisdom, as well as my internal and external beauty. Black women in community encouraged the growth of my spirit and voice. They all taught me about the power of kNOwledge. Despite all that I brought into the larger world,I was dismissed or diminished as a person. So, I learned to speak my "NO" as a manifestation of kNOwing my worth, often which resulted in exile. Working with my community of sisters taught me to view exile not as an exclusion, but as an opportunity to use my kNOwledge for a renewed life.

We must maintain relationships with our Black Christian sisters so we can rehearse our kNOwledge and our "NOs." When others demand a "yes" that threatens to degrade, demean, and destroy us, we offer our "NO," undergirding our courage to walk away from toxic environments and relationships. Thus, exile becomes an opportunity to walk toward freedom and thriving.

So, we who speak "NO" do not travel alone. In the company of our sisters, we will create sites of healing, power, and restitution. In these sacred spaces, we teach all who come to us about the necessity of life-affirming kNOwledge, and the wisdom to cultivate the power of "NO."

PRAYER: *God, help us to remember Vashti, kNOw our self-worth, and remember that we possess the power of the word "NO!" Amen.*

Rev. Dr. Imani-Sheila Newsome-Camara- After a long career in seminary education, Reverend Dr. Imani-Sheila Newsome-Camara serves as Christian Pastor and Spiritual Guide in Boston, Massachusetts.

SEASONS OF SISTERING

*I*n this section, Seasons of *Sistering* devotions are based on reflective messages that emanate from the biblical stories of women in need of sistering and community relationships during various times of life. *Sistering* is a sacred act, a sheltering, and a gateway to knowing and being known—loving and being loved—seeing and being seen during times when we need to be reminded that "we enter as one, but stand as ten thousand." Seasons of life are peppered with a multiplicity of seen and unseen circumstances ranging from a variety of momentous occasions, celebrations, transitions, to crisis, illness, death, and grief. *Sistering* in these seasons remind us we are not alone. Sistering allows women to dwell in the truth of who they are and know that Sista-girls, sojourners, friends, and ministry companions travel with us. The care, kindness, love, laughter, and the light of truth-telling and gentle reminders, from a sister through the ebb and flow of winter to the rebirth of spring, leisure of summer, and shifts during fall can help women of color persevere in ministry and leadership.

DR. DIANA CABEZAS

Seasons of Public and Prophetic Leadership

"… into the hand of a woman." (Judges 4:9)

As an immigrant Latina who pursued higher education and had a passion for spirituality, I always found it challenging to navigate spaces not designed for me and other women of color. In this journey, I have encountered and continue to confront socially- constructed systems created to undermine and disposition women of color in leadership roles. Yet, I remain close to God, igniting the commitment to my purpose. I reflect and recount the Deborah's of my life. Women who have gone before me, who have walked, trotted, and prophesied the victory that God will honor.

Deborah, a courageous leader stood in the gap and prophesied that victory over Sisera would occur under the hands of a woman. The Lord honored Jael, who without hesitation faced Sisera and took matters into her own hands. Deborah and Jael, whose posture toward God was of courage to be themselves, fearlessly and strategically confronted opposition and were honored by God, ultimately aiding victory for their people. You see, Deborah was faithfully doing what God positioned her to do, and Jael did so too. Each woman in their own space and life had a relationship with God, which positioned them to overcome the oppressive force often present in public and prophetic leadership.

There was and continues to be a divine thread, where Sisters knowingly or unknowingly influence the lives of each other. Some women have been trailblazing to cut through the pastures, fences, and cement that were purposely created to impede women of color from passing through. Yet, I encourage us to continue to pursue our paths just as Deborah and Jael did, being aware of the leading Spirit. Let's pray, prophesy, and confront that which faces us directly, as God will honor it. In our seasons, let's remain committed to our purpose and firmly stand our ground.

Our stories include women who long before prayed and prophesied, and it is in us to do the same. There are seasons to sow, water, prune, and reap the fruit of Divine labor. You will get to reap, and in the process, you'll be planting for the generations who will come after you. May we continue to be Divinely aligned to confront the embedded systemic layers that have been set out to prevent us from moving forward in ministry, academia, community, and spaces that God has positioned us to lead. May our posture be, to confidently stand, in who we are created to be in God so that the Divine thread pours courage, faith, and victory for those to come.

PRAYER: *Beloved God, like Deborah and Jael who stood firm in their calling, guide us in our leadership roles, that we may walk in the fullness of our destiny. Amen.*

Dr. Diana Cabezas resides in New Jersey and is committed to merging research, advocacy, and spirituality through an intersectional and strength-based lens to address health equity among underserved communities.

REV. TANEKI DACRES

I See You

"He sat down opposite the treasury, and watched the crowd putting money into the treasury. Many rich people put in large sums." (Mark 12:41)

*C*lang, clang, clang, goes the sound of heavy silver coins against the metal chests tossed in by the wealthy in the temple. Clang, clang, clang…I imagine that she stood at the entrance of the *Court of Women* waiting for the right moment. Waiting for the right moment to drop her two mites into the receptacle. Two mites, just about a penny's worth of money, but… there she was, waiting to give her all. She, like so many women of color, who have given their all in service to God and humanity, go unnoticed. And yet, she shows up…they show up…you show up. Clang, clang, clang, ping, there it goes her two mites, barely noticeable among the noise of the heavy coins that preceded hers.

No one thanks her. No one calls her by her name. No one acknowledges her sacrifice. Marginalized, alone, dismissed, and disregarded. And yet, time after time, she shows up…you show up. Sis, can you relate? There she was, a widow with two mites, sacrificially giving from depleted resources, but here's the beauty of the text: while she remained unappreciated and unseen by her community, she was seen by the one who mattered the most, Yeshua *Hamashiach.*

My Sister, when no one else sees you, God sees you and we see you. When you have poured out your all, sacrificially giving of your time and resources, know that God sees you, and we see you. When the burdens of life and ministry seem to weigh you down, and still you show up to love and serve, know that God sees you and we see you. When you pressed your way beyond doubts, fears and insecurities, just to be there, know that God sees you, and we see you. When you felt like giving up, but you still showed up anyhow, know that God sees you, and we see you. When you've spent nights crying and praying, praying and crying, and still show up, know that God sees you, and we see you. When you've ministered while broken, loved while heartbroken, served while disappointed, given your all without acknowledgment, know my Sister, that God sees you, we see you, and your sacrifice is not in vain.

PRAYER: *Almighty God, when my sister is feeling unappreciated, lonely and unnoticed, remind her that you are with her and you see her. Amen.*

Rev. Taneki Dacres is an ordained Minister, Publisher, Author, Workshop Facilitator and Writing Coach. As the

DR. PATRICIA GOULD-CHAMP

Seasons of Sacrifice and Service: Unnamed Women Caught, Brought – Released!

"...What do you say about her?" (John 8:5)

*I*t is virtually impossible for us to read the story of the woman caught in adultery without feeling and/or identifying with her pain. The woman caught in "adultery" is me, and perhaps all of my sisters! From the youngest to the oldest, through the many seasons in our lives, at one time or another, this has been our lived experiences. For we remember all too well those times when our own yearnings rendered us vulnerable. In this setup, this woman finds herself where many of us have found ourselves in the seasons of our lives – seen not as a human, but as a tool to be used by others for their own selfish purpose. Like this woman, many of us have been caught, brought, and released.

During a communal time of celebration, this woman is "caught" in adultery—an act that is deemed inappropriate, sinful, unacceptable, and worthy of death. As women, we've been in places where our mere seeking pleasure for ourselves led us to be "caught." We've gone through seasons in our lives when we felt trapped in situations, held captive to our circumstances, and caught in relationships that caused us to operate outside of our true commitments to God and self. In those seasons when our inner desires and needs caused us to be setup and used selfishly by others, sisters came to walk with us, and encouraged us as we struggled against our confinement. They inspired us to press through and not give up.

Not only is this woman "caught", but she is also "brought" to Jesus expecting she will be exposed, humiliated, and judged. All of us can remember those times when our names—our mistakes, our failures, our indiscretions – have been brought before others with the intent to shame us and kill us emotionally. It was in those seasons of our walk of shame that the sage sisters and the wise mothers walked with us and gave us the courage to live on. Their strength and steadfast sisterhood paved the way for our survival, and today, we continue this legacy.

Finally, this woman is released—"Go, and sin no more." Jesus releases her from who others have deemed her to be. Jesus releases her from the prison of her past to a redefined future. And the good news is that Jesus releases us as well. With Jesus, our seasons of growth and transformation are redefined. With Jesus, we too are released to "go and sin no more," to not allow our past to define us and hinder the future that has been prepared for us. The love and grace of Jesus continues to set us free and calls us from those seasons of being caught and brought to be released to new possibilities!

PRAYER: *Lord God, thank you for your grace that has sustained us, and for the awesome sisters who have been our shelter through life's many seasons.* Asé.

 Dr. Patricia Gould-Champ is the Founding Visionary and Former Senior Pastor of the Faith Community Baptist

A Handful of Faith: Obedience, Sacrifice, and Promise

" 'Bring me a little water…a morsel of bread in your hand.' She said, 'As the Lord your God lives…' she went and did…" (I Kings 17:12 and 17:15)

There are seasons of life where we are clouded by the circumstances surrounding us. In 2020 the world experienced a triple pandemic: anti-racism protests, economic devastation, and a COVID-19 virus, killing hundreds of thousands globally. For many, the basic need for survival overwhelmed and overtook us. There were tremendous losses experienced by many, and nameless faces and families who struggled to survive.

One can only imagine the widow of Zarephath, a nameless face in the crowd for whom we have no knowledge except that she was widowed with a son, and destitute in the midst of a three-year famine. This unknown woman received a miracle from God for her handful of faith. Imagine, honoring a request to provide water and bread when you have little, "Bring me a little water in a vessel, so that I may drink…bring me a morsel of bread in your hand." The widow of Zarephath wasted no time in honoring the request of the prophet Elijah…truly a handful of faith.

Imagine having already decided that death was upon you. Like so many mothers before and after her, she had stretched out what she had as far as she could. The meal. The oil. Her last. Their fate. Her resignation to the presumed obvious. Her obedience to God's divine plan for the prophet's life led to her sacrifice.

Without knowing much of her background, it is apparent that she was alone, and even in her misery, God used her faith. God saw her. While Scripture doesn't have a name for her, God knew her. God knows us too. In seasons of our lives when destitution resembles financial, family, relationship, equality and/or health struggles, we look to be seen by a God who knows us by name. While we may remain nameless to many, we can be assured, like the widow of Zarephath, that God sees our obedience, sacrifice, and service to Him. Our faithfulness, in times of destitution or a triple pandemic, can unlock the abundance of promises God has already prepared for us. Imagine, if God could save the Zarephathian widow and her son from death (v. 22), what He will do for you in your time of need.

As the God of grace sent Elijah to a resourceful, faithful woman on the verge of death, we too can exercise our faith and receive rescue. In the spirit of God's daughters, we move in the faith of servanthood and the belief of God's promises. In the Spirit, we move. This is our handful of faith.

PRAYER: *Lord, the heart and faith of your daughters belong to you. Use us, in community with others, through your Spirit to access your promise. Award our faith. Amen.*

Elder Tonetta Collins is Executive Pastor of Bible Way Ministries, International in

REVEREND DR. WANDA PAULK HOLDER

Ain't No Shame...

"The man said, "The woman you put here with me..." Then the Lord God said to the woman, "What is this you have done?" (Genesis 3:12-13)

When I was eight years old, I had a doll with three faces. A handle was located at the top of her head that allowed the head to be turned, changing the expression to a cry, frown, or smile. The doll was different and fun. In retrospect, I now realize this toy was more than fun. It provided a non-threatening way I could express how I felt at any moment. When I expressed my hurt with her face, I could avoid criticism or judgment. The adult responsible for the purchase probably thought it was cute, unaware that it provided an outlet for expression not necessarily granted to children. This was an era that believed in the family commandment "children are seen and not heard." No doubt, many children were scarred from this belief. You were made to feel ashamed of an emotion that was not a smile and a behavior not considered perfect. It is easy to understand how this" family commandment" was a subtle influence for self-criticism that gradually crippled confidence, and shame began to dominate.

Mother Eve retreated into shame responding to the comment from her husband and the question from her Creator. Being seen and not heard became the standard for her and the daughters to come. Women of color have been systemically pressed into hiding their feelings, using faces to appease others. Just as the doll was given as a toy, we have been given shame as a toy. Mother Eve can clearly speak to the claim of blame that cloaks us into shame. But I can hear her moaning through the ages and running after the generations of daughters who are still wearing this cloak. She shouts "STOP"! It is over—do not allow those who are at ground level of the cross place their yoke on you. Whatever then, now, and is to come, is forgiven and forgotten.

The shame face of brokenness, mistakes, and blindness have been and are still being made anew through the resurrection of Christ. You are still the beauty of your mother's womb. The tears you cry are only washing away those things that have obstructed your vision; the frown only symbolizes that you are readjusting your thoughts to a new thing; and your smile says "Amen."

PRAYER: *Gracious God, thank You that my mind, heart, and soul are no longer held hostage to the question, "What have you done?" from my family, mate, friends, and the church. It was never Your intent that I be smothered by the lips that condemned me. Lord let me not rehearse those moments that bruised me but celebrate my freedom from shame. In the Redeemer's name – Jesus – I Declare and Decree!*

Rev. Dr. Wanda K. Paulk Holder serves as a confidant, coordinator, intercessor and

REVEREND DR. LISA D. RHODES

Jesus Sees and Calls Women to Ministry

"Soon afterward he went on through cities and villages, preaching and bringing the good news of the kingdom of God. And the twelve were with him, and also some women…" (Luke 8:1-2)

*W*omen in ministry and religious leadership have a history of being on the margins, but at the center of his ministry, Jesus practices a theology of equivalence and makes space for their gifts. Against the social norms of the time, when it is considered politically incorrect, Jesus sees both women and men as essential to the kingdom. As Jesus walked throughout the cities and villages of Galilee, he called women from the ecclesial margins of patriarchal life to the center of religious leadership.

The twelve were with him, as well as some women. Mary Magdalene, mentioned by name and referred to by many New Testament scholars as a promoter of women's leadership, was an ordinary disciple who served in extraordinary ways. Often the target of rumors, scandal, and gossip, Mary Magdalene was an interpreter of Jesus's teachings, a potent spiritual guide, and prophetic visionary. Mary Magdalene played an important role in

Jesus' ministry and her name is forever etched in the cannon of biblical literature. The narrative and person of Mary Magdalene is distorted and misrepresented, as are stories of many women, yet she is remembered by name as one who Jesus called to step beyond the margins of female exclusivity imposed by culture and ecclesial systems, and serve God with confidence and courage.

Mary Magdalene, Joanna, Suzanna, and many others, struggled in life, just like each of us, and needed redemption from "evil spirits" or the internalized spiritual and emotional hurt that foster shame and prevent self-forgiveness. Others of us experience reoccurring anxieties and fears from childhood trauma, rejection, abandonment, intimate violence, and low self-esteem, and need to be redeemed by the love of God through the healing touch that only Jesus can bring. We put on our best face, hide behind masks, laugh the pain away, and take care of everybody but ourselves, and yet, Jesus sees us, offers us salvation, and makes space for each of us to walk alongside him in ministry.

Let us be as daring and audacious as the women who have a history of challenging traditional female roles ascribed by culture and religious institutions. Let us be as courageous as Jarena Lee, Sojourner Truth, Ella Pearson Mitchell, and Katie Geneva Cannon. Women like you, and women like me. Let us uphold the legacies of resistance and self- determination, and empower generations of women to walk with Jesus through the cities and villages, proclaiming and bringing the good news of the kingdom of God:; "For We Shall Not Be Moved."

PRAYER: Gracious God, as we continue the legacy of women who walked with Jesus, guide us with wisdom and discernment to always remember Your work of redemption is not limited to particular groups and persons, but to ALL who have faith. Amen and Asé

Reverend Dr. Lisa D. Rhodes- LCSW, DMin, ThD, (ABD), Executive Director, RISE Together Mentorship Network, Union Theological Seminary in the City of New York

A Love Note to the Sisters Who Stay.

"…she said to herself, If I only touch his garment, I shall be made well."
(Matthew 9:21)

*S*isters, let's face it. There are seasons of our lives filled with hardship and disappointment. There are seasons where it feels like every door closes in our face, every "yes" is a "no", and every dream gets deferred. In those seasons, it can be challenging to allow our friends into that space of disappointment. You know how it is—when your girl calls you hoping for good news, you do not want to disappoint. When she calls hoping you got the job, hoping your partner proposed, you got the house, you received a good health diagnosis, or hoping the situation y'all prayed about the night before has finally changed. When she calls, she's calling with the kind of hope you don't want to dash. Sometimes having to tell your girls, "No, it didn't happen" or "No, it didn't work out the way I hoped it would", can be more painful than the actual act of not getting what you've been praying for! If you're like me, you hate that look in the eyes of your sisters when they realize you are in pain.

Nevertheless, I've lived long enough to know that what we pray for doesn't immediately come to pass. Sometimes we find ourselves praying year after year   for change, but while we're praying, the folks around us are giving up hope. Sis, have you been there?

That's what makes the story of the woman with the issue of blood so powerful. She endured twelve years of a crisis yet she never lost her faith. She never lost her belief that healing would come. She pushed through the crowd, pushed through twelve years of pain, twelve years of disappointment, twelve years of no's, twelve years of embarrassment…and held on to hope.

Find sisters who stay…sisters who are willing to encourage you and sit with you in the horrors of your reality. Sisters who can handle your disappointment; friends who believe that healing is still possible. Find sisters who affirm you and remind you that your issue of blood does not define you, will not ruin your life, and will not have the last word.

My sisters, life is going to get hard—that is a certainty, but find some sisters who will stay and keep you going even when you don't get the answer you prayed for. They are a gift from God.

PRAYER: *Lord grant me the courage to invite my sisters into the fullness of my life's journey with boldness. Amen.*

This devotional is to encourage endurance in situations that take a while to change beyond your control. If you're in danger either physically or mentally, please hear this admonishment from me as a pastor and sister in Christ—never stay anywhere that your life is in danger.

Pastor Gabby Cudjoe Wilkes is a New York City pastor whose work is situated at

REVEREND GWEN R. ALDRIDGE

Seasons of Testing and Triumph

"And behold, a Canaanite woman from that region came out and cried, 'Have mercy on me, O Lord, Son of David; my daughter is severely possessed by a demon.' "(Matthew 15:22)

The euphoric feeling when one's life is progressing in the most positive way can lend itself to feelings of unimaginable joy.

During the good times, we float along in a dreamlike state enjoying our season of goodwill. We become more engaged, creating beautiful, and lasting memories. Our steps feel lighter and we smile just a little more often. As the morning breeze blows softly, we notice the beauty of God in creation, and we feel God's gentle kiss upon our cheeks. We see the leaves on the trees move to the rhythm of the wind and smell the fragrance of a freshly cut lawn adorned with beautiful flowers growing in the garden. Life is good, until it's not.

Suddenly, there's a disruption and a new reality appears...things change! The sense of jubilation begins to slip away, sometimes, little by little, and other times in one enormous explosion. Life as we know it transitions from delightful to dreadful, and the realization of this truth becomes wrapped in despair. The most difficult events in our lives make us wonder if those euphoric moments were real or just fantasy. We are poised in our humanness to quickly react. It is the Canaanite woman who offers an example of what it is to remain humble during crisis, to praise in the midst of pain, and to persevere through the storm despite of what is perceived as an uncompromising situation.

She maintains her focus, continuing her plea before the Lord, never giving up hope for deliverance. She leans in, letting her faith guide her purpose. It is the strength of our faith that gives rise to perseverance. It empowers us to focus our attention on the promises of God which facilitates inner peace and the process of moving forward. Sisters, as we journey between seasons, let us stay focused and never give up hope. As we travel through the valleys and mountain tops of life, let us remember to stay connected to God through our self-care and spiritual practices. Pray, meditate, and always remember we are not the culmination of our circumstances. We are beautifully and wonderfully made! Regardless of the season, we will, we shall, Rise Together!

PRAYER: *Lord, comfort my sisters. Give us the strength to endure the difficult seasons. Give us the peace, but most of all give us hope. Help us to feel your presence and see your revelation. Bless us in times of testing and triumph. We thank you for your grace, confident in knowing it is sufficient. In Jesus Name,*

Amen

 **Reverend Gwen R. Aldridge** is a graduate of Fuller Theological Seminary, Pasadena, California (MA Theology and Ministry) and Associate Minister, First Baptist Church, Pittsburg, California: Spiritual Director, Atrium Hospice

REVEREND DR. MYRNA THURMOND MALONE

Seasons in the Wilderness

And God heard the voice of the lad; and the angel of God called to Hagar
from heaven, and said to her, 'What troubles you, Hagar? Fear not...' "
(Genesis 21:17)

*A*s I reflect over my life, I am reminded of my experiences of despair...moments of great anguish—like being a single mom of two young children. I'm reminded of moments of despair when there wasn't enough time, food, or energy to get through the day, and junctures of fluctuating feelings between anger and hopelessness. I've had my Hagar season.

Hagar, a single Black mother and her son have run out of water and are now experiencing the fear of the wilderness of Beer-sheba, and the heaviness of being alone without options. As women of color in ministry, daily we face wilderness experiences. Experiences of despair and fatigue. Many of us are tired—tired of witnessing death and dying. Tired of being pushed aside. Like Hagar who was cut off from her systems of support, I have found myself contemplating my value and worth in ministry. Being tossed aside as a woman in ministry and being told I have no place or value is what many of us reflect on when we read this scripture. Hagar and

Ishmael were cast down because Sarah didn't want to share the inheritance with Hagar and her son. Abraham obeyed his wife and left them to be independent without resources.

Experiences of rejection can lead us to become weary and sorrowful, and cause us to weep. Although Hagar was obedient and conceived, she was met with harsh mistreatment, causing her to run away. In her wilderness experience Hagar was given a promise by God. Each time Hagar was in a place of despair God was present and demonstrated God's love and concern. In our places of despair, God was and is present.

Sometimes we may feel like we are alone; sometimes our situations can look impossible, but in our wilderness experiences God is present. God promises grace, hope, and love even as we feel anguish. Know that you have the power and freedom to cry out and release all that ails you, and God is your container to hold your lament. Keep your eyes fixed on God and know that when you are at your weakest, God will give you the strength to continue your race. Don't be afraid, lift up your head, and see the new things God is doing as you move through this experience of pain towards a path filled with new possibilities and new beginnings. You may be in the wilderness, but open your eyes, your heart, and lean on God who promises to meet you where you are.

PRAYER: *God our keeper and way-maker, we turn to You and trust You in our seasons of drought and wilderness experiences, knowing you are a God of the oppressed and marginalized. Amen.*

Reverend Dr. Myrna Thurmond Malone
Regional Spirituality Director in Atlanta, GA.

REVEREND NILDA ROMAN

Seasons of Second Chances

"...as I have dealt kindly with you, you also will deal kindly...and deliver our lives from death." (Joshua 2:1-13)

At some point during our journeys, we will come across unwanted or unexpected situations that frighten us and cause us to hide and seek safe spaces. I recall hiding under the bed during my childhood as I fled from my mother's wrath. I knew a well-deserved correction for lying was in the works, but I figured I could out-smart my mother. However, in her determination to find me, my mother searched every room and closet. To my misfortune, she would discover my sneakers at the bottom of the bed. So, what did she do? She would quietly retrieve the broom out of the closet, return to the bedroom, and poke me out from under the bed. I was forced to face the consequences, but at it the end of it, I was given a second chance to work on learning to tell the truth.

There is always a place of rescue when we are running from danger. In this passage God chose a resourceful woman named Rahab to hide spies on the rooftop of her home. This provided a second chance to recover from an unsafe predicament for both the spies and Rahab, who was labeled a harlot of the city of Jericho. The roof became their saving grace.

Whether it is personal losses, grief, unhealthy relationships, illness or other misfortunes, God's Spirit provides an opportunity that meets us in the midst of the chaos; and we are rescued miraculously into a better place. Rooftop experiences are divine dwelling places. These experiences permit us to be kept from further hurt and/or danger. These experiences bring about liberation.

Where is God sending you? God used Rahab an unlikely woman of color to usher in the way of Christ of the world. Be encouraged to find safe places that offer you comfort and strength. May we remain hopeful in trusting God for the second chances that provide shelter for our souls, minds and hearts; and may the Spirit affirm our protection as we search for peace and safety as we grow in grace.

PRAYER: *God, we give thanks in every circumstance, finding gratitude in the positive results and not the situation. Amen.*

Nilda Roman is currently the Chaplain/ Pastor at Luther Acres Assisted Living/Nursing Home in Lititz, PA.

GENERATIONAL SISTERING

*I*n this section, Generational *Sistering* reflects a mosaic of relationships across generations that offer models of *Sacred Sistering* through women in the biblical narrative, and Black history, as well as within families and friendships. Generational *Sistering* devotions offer unique coaching, mentorship, and the impartation of wisdom. These inspiring reflections help to edify, equip, and teach through generational story-telling, the wisdom, counsel, and power of faithful women of faith. From within the sacred text, women of color have inherited the voices and visions of women who embody and serve as exemplars, prioritize being prepared, and understand the significance and value of women in ministry and leadership. These sacred devotionals are timeless and reflect *Sistering* moments of tough love, truth-telling, and small rebukes, as well as lessons learned from younger sisters and friends, and visits with an elder. In honest, reciprocal, and mutually respectful relationships with sisters from various ages, who are younger, elders, or step out of the biblical and literary texts, generations of women have experienced enduring moments of love, guidance, friendship, and mentorship through and for women of color in ministry and leadership.

MELODY PANNELL, MSW, M. DIV., MACE

Be Prepared! It Can Cost You Everything

"Watch therefore, for you know neither the day nor the hour.." (Matt. 25:13)

*W*hen our dreams are nowhere in sight and the night is growing long, subconsciously we can "give up" and not prepare for the blessings that God has in store for us. Subconsciously we can become apathetic, drowsy with discouragement, and distant with discontentment. Therefore, we fail to plan ahead to ensure we are ready to receive the prophetic promises of God. We lose experiencing the excitement and the awakening that comes from looking forward to something special. Our spirits are lulled into a slumber and our creative energy is sapped. Our "big dreams" are diminished, and our vision is dimmed. We lose the strength to endure, perhaps, because deep down inside we do not believe that it will come to pass. Therefore, our "waiting" becomes just an empty act of obedience instead of a vibrant and active faith full of hope and anticipation.

In the parable, five bridesmaids were prepared for the arrival of the Bridegroom, and five bridesmaids were not prepared to endure waiting longer than their first batch of oil. The daylight diminished and as dust settled around them, the bridesmaids became drowsy. As the night grew long, their lights dimmed and soon they were asleep in the darkness, somewhere between what was and what was to come. Around midnight a shout awakened their hearts and quickened the spirits. The time had come! The waiting was finally over! Suddenly the Bridegroom was upon them and the promise was being revealed. Yet, only the ones with the extra flask of oil were prepared to trim their lamps and go out from the darkness to meet the Light.

The other five bridesmaids that had not prepared for the wait, were out of oil and time, even though this moment was all that they had been hoping for. Have you ever found yourself at risk for missing out on all that you had been waiting for? A lack of preparation can cost you years of hoping and dreaming for the desires of your heart. It can even negate and cancel out the time you spent faithfully and earnestly waiting for the promise. You see, the latter five bridesmaids did initially fill their lamps with oil. At some point there was a glimpse of faith, hope, and expectation. However, faith alone will not carry us into the promised land. We must utilize our faith, take action, and position ourselves for the wait. We must withstand the weariness so we can be ready for the Bridegroom who is on the way. God has not forgotten you and invites you to keep your oil lamps trimmed and burning brightly even in the midst of waiting.

PRAYER: *God of promise and hope, we ask that you bless us with wisdom and fortitude to endure until the end as we prepare ourselves to partake in the prophetic promises of our dreams. Amen.*

Minister Melody M. Pannell, a native of Harlem, NY, is a Mental Health Therapist, Professor and Founder of Destiny's Daughters Inc., currently residing in Harrisonburg, Virginia.

REVEREND LISA R. HARRIS LEE

When I See You: Carriers of the Promise

"And blessed is she who believed that there would be a fulfillment of what was spoken to her from the Lord." (Luke 1:45)

*A*re you familiar with the Zulu expression, Sawubona? It is part of a call and response greeting that embodies deeper seeing. The call, Sawubona translates to, "We see and value you. You are important to me." The response, Yebo, Sawubona translates to "We see you, too"; or Ngikhona, "Therefore I am seen." It is this kind of sight that gives Mary and Elizabeth the strength to stay on their paths of purpose.

The bond between Elizabeth and Mary shows a way generations of women can be supportive of each other. The kind of seeing Elizabeth and Mary offer each other does not happen in a passing glance but requires a persistent and patient gaze. There was an immediacy of response as the baby in Elizabeth's womb leaped for joy. Yet, their bond is also a sistering that lasts beyond one moment. It is born out of a common circumstance as they both prepare to give birth. Elizabeth and Mary gave each other something more than the natural eye can see. They "see" through listening with their hearts, and a stillness in the presence of God who reveals to them what words and sight cannot.

Imagine with me, more of what Mary and Elizabeth might have said during their visit together.

Mary - In you I see a safe place to be myself. You are where my heart, soul, dreams, gifts flourish with life-giving spirit and truth. When I see you the paces of my steps quicken to reach you because you are the place where love, understanding, joy and wisdom dance together.

When I see you, I know you are the one who carries the promise that prepares the way for the Promise I carry. I am encouraged to deliver the Word of God in its fullness.

Elizabeth – When I see you, I see the God in you. Who you carry brings light to the shadows. When I see you, I must exclaim with a shout—not a whisper—"God is with us! Finally, the Promised One has been conceived!" When I see you, my purpose is fulfilled…

Elizabeth and Mary in chorus – Together, we are stronger and more fully ourselves. We stand together at the crossroads of grace, a God-ordained intersection that will forever cause our stories to be woven together for the world that God so loves.

PRAYER: *Promise-Making God, help us to see each other and cheer one another on, in a way that brings life to us and to the world. Amen.*

Rev. Lisa R. Harris Lee — National Director of Healing and Transforming Communities, American Baptist Home Mission Societies, King of Prussia, PA. Serving with ministry leaders in the United States and Puerto Rico.

Blood Ties: Sistering Among Siblings

"Martha, Martha, you are anxious and troubled about many things…" (Luke 10:41)

*H*ow do I write about the perils of being "worried and distracted" while I am myself "worried and distracted"? I am Martha through and through, and have worn the title proudly. How dare anybody, but especially my sister, sit at anybody's feet, Jesus's included, while I'm working my fingers to the bone. Yes, I have been a Martha apologist; I have joined her in being salty with Mary. Truth be told, I have even side-eyed Jesus for rebuking Martha instead of making Mary get off her "rusty dusty" to set the table.

On its surface, this text appears to pit two sisters against one another, and lodges a man, albeit Jesus, right smack in the middle of it all. The makings of a reality show of epic proportions, replete with cat fights and intermittent "bleeps," for certain. At first blush, the passage seems to run afoul of any semblance of sistering, let alone generational sistering. But herein lies a lesson I learned from my own sister and her generation.

Taylor is 20 years younger than I am. When she was born, I was already grown and in college. She never lived in a home without a microwave or cable. She's never known a world where popcorn options were limited to the stovetop, and television ended at midnight with the Star-Spangled Banner. I have judged her generation for not knowing what it means to exercise patience, a generation constantly distracted by the pings of their gadgets. But unlike me, Taylor learned the value of living in the moment with a level of intentionality I seem reluctant to muster. Perhaps inheriting a world full of distractions forced her to learn the art of presence.

Taylor's ability to live in the moment was no more poignant than when our father was in hospice care several years ago. I was Martha, worried and distracted by what life would be without my dad; she was Mary, sitting at his feet, savoring the time they had left. I rarely felt resentment toward her because her presence brought both of them much joy and because my sister stood to lose her father before she turned 30, while I'd had him in my life almost 50 years, upon reflection, I wish that between seeing to his physical needs, I had spent more time sitting at my dad's feet, gleaning the wit and wisdom that only an old preacher can muster. Those are moments I cannot get back.

If you have Martha-like tendencies as I do, I pray you will grow to learn the value of not only doing, but being—being present for those you love, and with the One who calls us friend. I am grateful for younger sisters who have shown me the way.

PRAYER: *Gracious God, You are present with us even when we are distracted by and worried about what we are doing. Thank you for sisters who show us how to be present with each other and with you. Amen.*

Kathryn V. Stanley, J.D., MRL, an educator, writer and editor, works in ministry at Ebenezer Baptist Church in Atlanta, GA.

REVEREND DR. LISA ALLEN-MCLAURIN

Change Agents of History: Stand Your Ground

"...Give to us a possession among our father's brethren." (Numbers 27:4)

*B*orn in poverty, Fannie Lou Hamer sharecropped on Mississippi plantations her entire life until she was fired for attempting to vote. Hamer worked with the Student Nonviolent Coordinating Committee (SNCC) and the Southern Christian Leadership Conference (SCLC) to register African Americans to vote, enduring brutal assaults, and unjust incarcerations.; Nevertheless, she persisted. In 1964, Hamer co-founded the Mississippi Freedom Democratic Party and gave a televised testimony advocating for integrated delegations, and in 1971 helped co-found the National Women's Political Caucus.

In a similar spirit, by age fifteen, Prathia Hall was determined to join the Civil Rights Movement. She became one of the first women field leaders of SNCC. She registered African Americans to vote during the '60s, was jailed, shot at, and threatened constantly. Nevertheless, she persisted. While teaching in freedom schools and speaking in mass meetings, Prathia is credited for first uttering the famous phrase, "I have a dream." She is the first women ordained by the American Baptist Association.

Like the determination of Hamer and Hall, Stacey Abrams became a change agent of history. In 2018 she ran for governor of the state of Georgia. A state representative for several years, Abrams was well aware of the political climate and uphill battle she would face; nevertheless, she persisted. Tainted by claims of intentional voter suppression, Abrams refused to concede, instead she founded Fair Fight Action, a nonprofit organization dedicated to voter rights advocacy. Abrams is credited with leading the change in Georgia's and America's political landscapes, with over 80,000 net voter registrations in 2020.

These women exhibited extraordinary courage, wisdom, and agency, reminiscent of the daughters of Zelophehad. Numbers 27:1-11 recounts the narrative of these remarkable sisters who came to Moses and Eleazar, questioning the law and demanding to be counted as rightful heirs to their deceased father's inheritance, an unprecedented request in a patriarchal society. Because of their persistence, Moses took the case before God who affirmed their request and commanded Moses to institute an immediate change in the legal systemic structure.

Like the daughters of Zelophehad, Hamer, Hall, and Abrams refused to accept prevailing status quos. Though centuries of legal and cultural inequities stood guard, they did not allow established precedents to deter necessary changes. They preached, pressed, and persisted as change agents, fighting against systemic injustice until new precedents were set, not solely for personal benefit, but for the liberation and empowerment of entire communities. My sister, keep preaching, pressing and persisting. You are the change agent who is called to work to dismantle systems of oppression, no matter the risks or outcomes. You are the shoulders upon which future generations stand. Your voice matters, your ministry matters, and you matter.

PRAYER: *Blessed Warrior-Mother-Spirit, Give us courage, wisdom, and the persistent spirit of your change agents, helping us to find claim, and raise our voices for the uplift of your people. Yeshua Hamashiach, Jesus, the Anointed One. Amen and Ase.*

The Reverend Dr. Lisa Allen-McLaurin is the Helmar E. Nielsen Professor of Church Music and Worship at the Interdenominational Theological Center in Atlanta, Georgia, and the Coordinator of Practical Ministries for the Sixth Episcopal District of the Christian Methodist Episcopal Church.

Blaze the Trail

"Give to us a possession among our father's brethren." (Numbers 27:4)

Trailblazers are visionaries who can imagine a world much better than the one they were given. Therefore, they take steps to bring that world to life. They find a way to chisel a threshold wide enough for not only themselves, but for those who will come after. These five women, Mahlah, Noah, Hoglah, Milcah, and Tirzah, were left with few choices. Either they would stand silently and watch as their inheritance was given away to some undeserving man, or they would take a stand. In the midst of grief and facing the loss of their estate, they chose to stand united. They stood boldly before piercing eyes and dared to ask for their inheritance.

The sisters standing together is an important detail of this text. They needed each other, the younger sisters needed the elder sisters' wisdom and foresight while the elder sisters needed imaginative curiosity and wonder that defines youth. Innovation does not occur in a vacuum, it is cultivated through creative conversations, mentorships, and "sister-friends" who see you and push you towards your passions.

Who sisters you when you face challenges? Who steps in with godly wisdom and encouragement? How have you sistered to others as they blaze trails? What are some qualities a sister should possess?

The label of trailblazer is rarely sought after; it is a title that is hard-won and more likely given after one has lived their life. While we may not see ourselves currently as trailblazers…we are. Like the five sisters in our scripture, we must make the decision to either wait or find the strength to face the obstacles in front of us.

When that time comes, here are a few essentials to remember:

- We are not self-made. We are, because of those who have come before us; those who have helped to cultivate our paths. May we always look back and remember the shoulders we stand on.

- We must find people who understand and know how to give wisdom on our journey.

- "As iron sharpens iron" we need iron friends and companions who will celebrate us as we flourish, love us when we're down, and motivate us when we feel like giving up.

- We must always write our why and keep it with us. Our memories are short when breaking barriers.

Finally, when the negative voices raise up we must remember God has called us. The vision would not have been placed within us if it was not God's will. God's timing is not our timing.

PRAYER: *Creator God, make clear the path and my vision. Amen!*

Rev. La Donna Williams cultivates space for healing, curiosity, and hope through storytelling and performing arts.

When Love Overcomes Bitterness

"...call me Mara (bitter)..." (Ruth 1:20)

The story of Ruth and Naomi begins with their shared tragedy and demonstrates the power of generational sistering to provide healing love and support through a biblical narrative.

One of the greatest, natural examples of when love overcomes bitterness is when we see people, who have suffered an insurmountable grief experience, be surrounded and embraced by people who love them. These moments capture us at our lowest points in life. Moments that solidify humanity's irreparable brokenness. These are moments filled with anger, profound sadness, gut-wrenching, and heart-shattering pain. These moments exist in the lives of women who have lost children due to gun violence.

I have been able to see this up close on more than one occasion. The unfortunate side of it all is that I had to witness women live out their most horrendous nightmares, to which there are no words of comfort. One incident in particular was when a childhood friend of mine was forced to say goodnight to her nineteen-year-old son. The time that followed was one of the most traumatic and torturous seasons of her existence.

Reconnecting with her during that season allowed me to witness a tremendous outpouring of love and support from everyone who loved her, especially her two remaining children. Because she allowed herself to open up to receive this love, and not reject it, she was able to survive. Their love helped her to overcome bitterness created by this extreme loss. God's infinite wisdom inserted a silver lining which is the immeasurable, unstoppable, outpouring of love.

This is the same love we saw exhibited through Ruth's refusal to leave Naomi's side. In Ruth 1:1-18, we are introduced to Naomi, Ruth and Orpah, and their overwhelming loss. We were also introduced to Ruth's immovable love for Naomi, who said goodnight to her husband and both of her sons. This love was used to provide the healing that Naomi so desperately needed. By the end of the book of Ruth, we have the privilege to witness Naomi's healed heart lead her as the matriarch, and guide Ruth to become the bride to Boaz.

If there is anything that we can take away from this devotional, it would be: Always have enough humility to receive genuine love when offered from someone who is in an ancillary position to yours. It may turn out to be the gift of a blessing that keeps on giving.

PRAYER: *Lord, we thank you for this opportunity to come together and experience what generational sistering can be like. Help us to continue to overcome bitterness with love. In the mighty name of Jesus, Amen.*

Professor Chanta' N. Barrett is an Adjunct Professor at Lincoln University in PA and, as an Entrepreneur, leads CN Productions focusing on theological and educational creative media cnichole.org.

PRAYERS FOR OUR SISTERS

*I*n this section, women of color recognize that prayers have always been and continue to be critical for inspiration, healing, hope, and sustaining our *Sisters* of the diaspora in life, leadership, and ministry. *Prayers for Our Sisters* offer a multifaceted continuum of Holy Spirit led, awe-inspiring words of gratitude, praise, and thanksgivings to God for the blessings of forgiveness, deliverance, strength, and perseverance. Women in ministry and leadership open their hearts to pour forth prayers that embody the realities of their day-to-day lives. What a wonder to meditate on Scripture and call on the name of the Lord. These powerful prayers by our Sister Sojourners in ministry are lifted for the protection of our children and communities, and for the divine guidance needed whenever women of color in ministry walk into places of worship and leadership. As the final section of our *Sacred Sistering Devotional*, P*rayers for Our Sisters* are of deep and abiding significance to every woman leader of color who dares to believe in a faithful God who will empower and equip her for ministry. The prayers are a reminder of how we are all weaved together through pain and healing, tears and laughter, time and continent, with the tenacity to RISE up.

REVEREND TONI BELIN INGRAM

Prayer for Wisdom- Prayers for Effective Leadership

"... the leaders took the lead in Israel..." (Judges 5:2)

God, the One of wisdom who shakes the earth, makes the mountains quake, and the clouds pour down water.

We, Your daughters, are in awe of all the ways You are God. We are reminded that during battles we are not alone. We praise You, that in You, all things are possible. We praise You, God, for the myriad of ways You consistently have blessed and sustained Your daughters that we might bless and sustain others. We praise You, Lord, and are reminded that at the right time, You provide for us the instruction, the power, the resources, and the people we need to accomplish the goals You have set for us.

God, for the new leaders that have been set apart for this season, we pray a supernatural anointing that would fall afresh as they lead generations to You. Teach us discernment and wisdom we would follow even when the honor will not be ours. God, when others sin against us, raise those among us that would thwart the enemy. Share with us, God, the measure of Your justice that makes us ready for war. God, remind us, that the work we do is to Your Glory so that generations will never forget that You alone are God.

Equip us to always stand against the enemy. In the times in which we live we need Holy Ghost Power to inspire and instruct, provide and protect, heal and restore, and lift and set free. Help us God, to RISE daily in the strength of Your love and walk humbly in Your power, that there will be peace in our land, we pray Amen.

"I used to define myself by the roles I performed for others. I stopped this foolishness because it hid my brilliance, strength and beauty." **The Reverend Toni Belin Ingram, D.Min.,** Presiding Elder, Augusta North District African Methodist Episcopal Church

Prayer to Walk in Confidence

"Is any cheerful? Let him sing praise." (James 5:13)

God of Strength, God of Peace, God of Love,

Be with my Sisters as they, we, walk the paths you have called us to walk. Paths which will cause us to enter difficult places and spaces, where at times even the "allies" will try to mute our voices and silence our actions. Spaces where some will only acknowledge our voices after a man has co-signed on it. Spaces where shallow flattery will be used to try and get us to stand down and get in line with the voice of the patriarchal status quo. Spaces where when we press on to be heard, we will be met with retaliation, both overt and subtle. In these moments, God...

Remind us that long ago, you called women to lead your people as warriors, caregivers, prophets, and so much more as when you called Deborah to lead her people to fight back against those who oppressed them.

Remind us our steps have been ordered, and you have divinely purposed us to lead paradigm shifts, reimagine the status quo, and tear down man-built walls which seek to maintain the power and the position of a few to the detriment of most.

Remind us, when self-doubt starts to overtake us, that you are with us and will continue to strengthen us so we will walk our paths in confidence, no matter the foe.

Remind us so we will be able to walk not just in confidence but also in peace, knowing our leadership, our voices, are invaluable and cannot be substituted.

Remind us that it is precisely because we are women that our voices carry such tremendous power that cannot and will not be silenced, muted, or denied! Women are often forced to grapple with all three of these and declare power over them.

In the mighty name of Jesus. Amen.

Min. Charisse A. Nelson is a Minister | Educator | Leader | Catalyst, pushing for the radical changes needed to energize

GENISE A. REID, ED.D.

Lord, Equip Us.

"The peasantry ceased in Israel, they ceased until you arose, Deb'orah, arose as a mother in Israel." (Judges 5:7)

*A*lmighty God, please shine Your light through the work of all women in leadership, just as You did through Israel's judge Deborah.

We ask You to grace all women in leadership with the experience of Your presence, so that their lives can be an expression of Your character.

We ask for Your unlimited resources to be provided to women in leadership; may they be fully equipped for doing the work You have called them to do.

We pray that Your wisdom would be impressed upon the hearts of women leaders, giving them clarity and certainty of all You have said in Your Word.

We pray that as Deborah's leadership ushered in forty years of peace, so may women's leadership in our time be the pathway to peace.

For the honor of Your Name please grant Your presence, Your resources, and Your wisdom to girls and young women who will become future leaders. Grant each one a strength of faith to overcome the trials of life in their youth. Please bless them with peaceful homes and godly role models, that they might lead well in the years to come.

Lord God, You included Deborah in the canon of Scripture as an example of a leader who received Your divine direction and acted with effectiveness. We ask for You to continue this holy impartation: Your blessing of divine direction in modern-day times for every woman You place in leadership. We pray this in the name of our Lord Jesus, who reigns with You and the Holy Spirit, One God, now and forever. Amen.

 **Genise A. Reid, Ed.D.** serves as Part-Time Program Manager for the RISE Together Mentorship Network.

DIANA BIEN-AIME, PH.D.

Healing Wounds Between Sisters

"Then God opened her eyes..." (Genesis 21:19)

God, Your Word reminds us to wait on You and be of good courage. As You promise to reveal Yourself in the birthing of life and gifts within us, may we be careful to give thanks to You for the sisters You place around us for a time such as this. May we forgo impatience and feelings of helplessness and begin to view our physical bodies, and spiritual presence as bearers of Your promises. May we cast off the heavy load of guilt and distressing thoughts about our beloved sisters that do not align with thoughts that are true, honorable, just, and pure.

Forgive us for expressing emotions of anger, jealousy, fear or haughtiness that may have harmed our relationship. Fill us with the fruit of the Spirit that we may rejoice and be faithful to each other, good and kind to one another. Fill us with the Spirit that we may be peaceable and patient with each other, gentle with each other, self-controlled and forgiving of one another. Above all, let us love each other as faithful bearers and speakers of Your powerful Word over one another.

We are thankful for resolution when enmity arises. We will do as You have asked us to do, for You called us a royal priesthood, a holy nation. We lift up our voices and weep and wail, for You have reconciled us one to another. We shall not be afraid. Our eyes are open, and for that, we say thank You God. In Jesus' name. Amen.

 **Diana Bien-Aime-Garrett, Ph.D.** is an Assistant Professor of

Trusting God for the Promise

"My heart exults in the Lord…" (I Samuel 2:1)

Gracious God of hope, I come before you layered in life's uncertainties. Nevertheless, just as Hannah, I am a daughter of faith. Though struggles and brokenness often tease my faith, You gently push through the cracks of my soul to encourage me to "Trust." While those I love and serve disregard me, failing to comfort my heart and soul, I admit it is difficult to see you Lord. There are subtle rejections because I am a brown woman with a bold tongue. Sometimes family, friends and even the church folks would rather disregard my truth and attempt to crush my spirit. Because your grace and mercy are faithful and sufficient, I still stand.

Amid tribulations, You lovingly propel me towards the pinnacle of knowing myself; You allow my silhouette of confidence to RISE; I stand with Hannah and all daughters to embrace dignity and celebrate our integrity. Even when the enemy pursues, trying to make us doubt your promise, You admonish us to "Trust." You impregnated Hannah with the promise of Samuel. You continue to impregnate your daughters with passions to be birthed. Glory to your name! You are the God of the impossible. I stand assured that trusting You gives me hope and vision. You have given me sight of my gifts, anointing, and purpose.

Thanks be to You that the view of who I am is not dimmed from the rejection of family, friends, and the church. Yes! Compassionate God, You let me see "Her." Her name is WORTHY! She stands stronger than ever before. So yes, I will "Trust" You! Through tears, I will "Trust" you! Through the ignorance and the abandonment of simple humane care, I will "Trust" You. I will "Trust" Your View of Me! And "She" is Beautiful. In Jesus' Name it is Done and Amen!

Reverend Dr. Wanda K. Paulk Holder serves as a confidant, coordinator,

REVEREND MARISA D. WHITE, M.A., CCC-SLP

Prayer of Surrender

"The adversaries of the Lord shall be broken to pieces; against them he will thunder in heaven." (1 Samuel 2:10)

God, as Your daughters, we thank You for pouring out Your love towards us, for Your mercies are new every day. Our source of power is the Holy Spirit and the Word of God. Our lips release the Word of God through faith. Our warfare originates in the heavens. We bind what is already bound in the heavens. We loose what is already loosed in the heavens. We abound in the fragrance of Your deliverance, for no weapon formed against us shall prosper, and every tongue that rises against us in judgment shall be condemned. God, You have revealed Your glory in my life; I pray now that You move in the same manner over these sisters. Let Your righteousness be exposed to all.

God, only You give life; and we, like Hannah, cry out now, surrendering anything that contaminates the birthing of life and new possibilities. Hannah prayed from her heart, and her lips did not move. Out of the chambers of our hearts, we plead for Your power through the proclamation of Your Word. May Your Word saturate and flow in and through us. A new birth is necessary. God, we pray for Your hand of mercy over our wombs, from which all creative energy flows. May You begin to heal us from the inside out, binding up and casting out all spirits that would attempt to keep us from giving birth to the visions, dreams, and possibilities You have provided. God, we cast down false narratives about ourselves placed on us by people, leaders, and the church, that may hinder our expectant delivery.

God, we depend You to be our strength as we overcome all fear: leaning not to our own understanding, but acknowledging You as You direct our paths. Hear our prayers both audible and silent. You shall continually be the source of our joy, God, for we know that You do all things well and in Your time. God, we surrender all. Amen

 Reverend Marisa D. White, M.Div, M.A. CCC-SLP, resides and serves the

CHANTA' N. BARRETT M.DIV

Prayer of Wrongdoing: Truth Telling-Prayers
for Healing Relationships

"… my mouth will utter truth…" (Proverbs 8:7)

*L*ord, You know this life can be complicated and there are times when speaking the truth means hurting the people we love and no matter how much we try to season it with love, it still won't be enough to repair the damage that may be done. In the hard moments like the loss of a loved one, or position, or a health diagnosis, Lord, allow me to lean on you and trust you with my heart.

Lord, I come to You asking for the strength and courage to continually tell the truth. I ask that You allow us to despise wickedness, and let our lips possess the sweet drippings of truth. Allow that speech to be an affirmation and a confirmation to what You have already spoken to us during our quiet time together. Allow us to lay aside falsehood, and speak truth to each other, for we are members of the same body. Allow us to speak truthfully to one another, and bless us to have a heart to receive that truth no matter how hard.

Lord Jesus, touch us to live peacefully with one another, and to speak the truth to each other; evaluating every situation, with truth and love, that our hearts may trust in each other. Bless us to be strong in You, and possess all manner of braveness, because we will need courage to live a life guided by truth-telling. Lord, grant us the courage to speak the truth, courage to live the truth, and courage to stand for the truth.

Lord, I say thank You again, for everything and I ask all of these things in Jesus' name. Amen.

Professor Chanta' N. Barrett is an Adjunct Professor at Lincoln University in PA and as an Entrepreneur leads CN

REVEREND DR. CATHERINE E. WILLIAMS

Prayer for Our Children

"He will guard the feet of his faithful ones; but the wicked shall be cut off in darkness…" (1 Samuel 2:9)

God…Mother God, we come to You on behalf of our children. The pains of childbirth have given way to pains of grief and worry. We tell ourselves not to worry, but worry has become our constant companion because we know our children are constantly endangered. We want to protect them from random acts of evil and spiteful acts of hatred because of the color of their skin. We bring our worries to You.

As Hannah brought her young son to the temple and left him in Your care, we bring our children to You in prayer. Hold them. Protect them. Guide and direct them. Like You did for Samuel, place godly people in our children's lives who will teach them to recognize Your holy voice. Train their eyes to see You and their hearts to turn towards You. O God, no one is holy like You, the God who brings down the proud and exalts the humble. Do not let evil prevail over our children's lives, O God.

Strengthen us, as their mothers, grandmothers, aunts,

godmothers, and all who represent Your mothering presence in their lives, to persevere in our prayers for them, knowing there is nothing they can ever do that will separate them from Your love. May we follow Hannah's trust as we release them into Your holy care.

This we ask in the name of Jesus, the Son, who knows our joys and our sorrows, and who is now interceding with us for our children. It is in this holy name we pray, Amen and Amen.

Oh God, If Hannah could entrust her only child into the hands of an aging priest who was not even a relative, help us to entrust our children into the hands of You, their true Parent, who loves them more than we ever can.

Reverend Dr. Catherine E. Williams is Assistant Professor of Preaching and

REV. DR. LISA D. RHODES

We Praise Your Name

"All the women went out after her with tambourines and with dancing."

And Miriam sang to them..."

*D*ear God, we enter this moment of prayer empowered by the memory of women who carry in their hearts a song of praise, and express through dance, jubilance because You have delivered them from their enemies. The Israelites, fled from Pharaoh's army, confronted the depths of the Red Sea, and You opened a safe path for them to cross on dry ground; but their oppressors, You destroyed. You are El Shaddai, God Almighty, and we praise Your Name.

For when we have confronted insurmountable challenges in the wilderness of life, and cried out in great fear like the Israelites, You parted the turbulent Red Seas of trepidation, turned our dread to deliverance and our wilderness to wonder. So, in the spirit of solidarity with Miriam, the women who followed her, and all our Sisters across the globe, We Praise You with tambourines and dancing. When our backs were against the walls of oppression, You sent forth Your Word — "The Lord will fight for you...You have only to keep still." Therefore, every mountain You've gotten us over, and every valley You've seen us through, we offer You a song of hallelujah, and a dance of praise.

Dear God, we praise Your name for endowing us with fortitude to press when we could not see our way; and for walking with us through and beyond the Red Seas of invisibility, marginalization, and disempowerment because of gender bias. So although life and ministry sometimes overwhelm us and our weariness wears us down, with the fruit of our lips, the swaying of our hips, and the lifting of our hands, We Praise Your Name, Regardless.

Amen and Asé!

 Reverend Dr. Lisa D. Rhodes, LCSW, DMin, ThD, (ABD), Executive Director, RISE Together Mentorship Network,

REVEREND BRITTINI L. PALMER

Prayer of Dance and Release

"...With timbrels and dancing. And Miriam sang to them: "Sing to the LORD, for he has triumphed gloriously; the horse and his rider he has thrown into the sea." (Exodus 15:20-21)

God, let me dance like Miriam!

Let my sisters and I dance in the face of our enemies as they oppose us. When they treat us inferior, let your love protect us. We pray for wisdom, balance, and strength to be free when the world tries to persecute us. God, let us be able to release when evil knocks on our doors. Let us dream a new song in the middle of blue waters and clear skies.

Help Us!

Help us get through days of destruction and cloudiness. When large armies try to deny our humanity, give us permission to sing and dance, laugh and love, risk and wait, love and leave. God, we move our bodies to the speed and rhythm of Your holy tunes. We clap our hands and invoke freedom over our bodies and minds. God, death is all around, yet I dance. I am protected.

We are protected!

God, I dance and tap my foot three times to thank you, the Holy One, for what will happen. We dance and tap our feet three times thanking the ancestors for our victorious celebration.

I let go…we let go of limitations we've placed on ourselves. I let go…we let go of the lies we believed about ourselves. We exhale and hurl our doubts into the ocean. We declare we will LIVE even in the midst of evil. Oh God of deliverance, we declare our freedom, choices, and agency never ends. Let us always find space to celebrate and dance our way through our daily emancipation.

Asé and Amen.

 Reverend Brittini L. Palmer is a freedom writer, public theologian, and Communications Consultant, who currently

INIVA NGAKA

Prayer to Accept God's Call Against the Odds

"For behold, henceforth all generations will call me blessed;" (Luke 1:48)

A Prayer of surrendering that can be recited daily. Inspired by Mary's Song of Praise.

*O*h God, give me the courage to say yes when you call. Help me to recognize; trust your voice among the multitudes.

Like Mary, place within me an abiding faith, an eagerness to serve.

Guide my sister each step of the way, even as she might hesitate.

Give my sister a spirit of boldness; able to conquer all fears, to silence any naysayers.

Let your glory be manifested on the four corners of this earth.

Through our sisterhood, may your presence shine forth, softening hearts, transforming each one into her best self.

May this prayer remind us to radiate light and send forth love when in the presence of our sisters and all others.

Iniva R. Ngaka is a logophile and an educator who finds joy in serving as a public

REV. LASHUNDRA D. RICHMOND

A Prayer for Birthing Divine Vision

"My soul magnifies the Lord and my spirit rejoices in God my Savior."

(Luke 1: 47)

Thank you God for including women from the very beginning. Thank you for guiding us on how to birth your divine vision. A vision which includes the purpose and position of women in creation. We thank you that despite circumstances and humble beginnings, you chose us, like you chose Mary, and our soul magnifies the Lord.

We thank you for being the giver of every good and perfect gift. We boast of your limitless mercy and arousing strength that catapults us into living abundant lives filled with dreams. Help us Lord to see past our own frailties and the social constructions of race, class, and gender. Help us to not be defined by stereotypes, biases, and prejudices, but rather the visions that you've placed over our lives. When this world isn't always kind to us, we pray that you will be our guiding light as we attempt to shine light upon others.

God help us to never discount what you've deposited inside of us. He who is mighty has done great things, for each of us. May our hearts continue to rejoice. May we find peace in the truth of Your Word. You chose me. You chose us. May we continue to always give you the glory, shout praises to Your Name, honor Your presence in our lives, and strive to make Your Name great. May there always be a melody in our hearts and a song on our lips of your goodness and unwavering love. May we sing cheerfully of your promises and favor shown towards us.

God, we pray that our eyes continue to be fixed towards Heaven. This prayer we seal and sing in our hearts always, Amen.

Rev. LaShundra D. Richmond Founder-The Destiny House San Diego, CA.

MONIQUE J. FORTUNÉ

Tending to Our Gardens

"I am very dark, but comely... they made me keeper of the vineyards; but, my own vineyard I have not kept!" (Song of Solomon 1:5-6)

*M*other Father God. I thank You. I am BLACK and BEAUTIFUL. Forgive me for the times when I abused myself with self-doubt and self-denial. I remember to care for myself by loving You, loving myself, and the sepia daughters of the new Jerusalem kissed by the sun.

Way-maker, as Black Womxn, we stand in the garden of intersectionality - race, class and gender that has contributed to black women's oppression through the ages. The empire shows up and tries to destroy, disrespect, demean and diminish our gardens. We rebel against the weeds of empire and tend to our gardens by providing the light of resilience, the soil of hope, and the water of resurrection.

Black Womyn find themselves at the mercy of abusive circumstances—health disparities, economic injustices and social and cultural stereotypes. We are not taking care of everyone else and neglecting ourselves. We are not the "strong, black woman" who denies her own hurt and pain. We are not hypersexual women available for anyone's desire. We are WOMEN faithfully and lovingly tending to our gardens. God, we thank Alice Walker for reminding us that our gardens were first tended and nurtured by our mothers, grandmothers, and mother ancestors that prayed for the flourishing of gardens yet to be.

Creator, let us tend to our gardens with a magnificent, urgent, and courageous love. Let us breathe anew with each new morning. Let us exhale with peaceful rest at night. Let us tend to our gardens with well-earned tears and robust laughter. Creator, let us bask in Your sunshine, dance in Your wind, play with Your earth and swim in Your waters. Let us take time to restore and refresh. Let it be so. Amen.

Monique J. Fortuné, a New York City native, is president of *Fortuné and Associates* teaching public speaking, organizational

COLLEEN BIRCHETT, PH.D.

Prayer to Resist Racial and Gender Injustice

"I am very dark, but comely, O daughters of Jerusalem…"

(Song of Solomon 1:5)

O h, Great Artist of the Universe, we pray to thank you. As beneficiaries of your creativity, we thank you for the artistry of your hands and the breath of your nostrils. For you have shaped and formed us into a beautiful bouquet that reflects the diversity of your creation. We thank you, Oh God, that our beauty radiates from within and is also embodied in communities of color. Yet, since we are so often abused and oppressed, our beauty is hidden by social injustice and we need the power of your Holy Spirit to face the challenges of the day.

Many of us are struggling to cope with untimely deaths of loved ones. We continue to lose others to police violence and health disparities that disproportionately impact communities of color. Oh, Lord, we need you. We need your power to fight to protect our right to vote. We need to remove toxic wastes from our environment and drinking water. We need your power to educate and equip our young people to succeed and live their best lives. We need the compassion of your love to create safe spaces and protect our seniors. Oh Lord, Our God, be with our village, with each of us, mothers and grandmothers, teachers and community leaders, and all who are village keepers for communities of color. Give us wisdom, teach us how to balance ministry with motherhood and marriage, and care for our personal and family needs.

Oh Lord, in the midst of these challenges, help us to carry the sweet scent of your Holy Spirit into the spaces where you have placed us. Amen and Asé!

Colleen Birchett, Ph.D., M.S., M.Div., is Assistant Professor of English, New York

DR. VALERIE CARTER SMITH

A Prayer for Our Gardens

"Do not gaze at me because I am swarthy, because the sun has scorched me.
My mother's sons were angry with me, they made me keeper of the vineyards;
but, my own vineyard I have not kept!" (Song of Solomon 1:6)

*G*od, my God, who moved from the beginning along the face of the dark and deep abyss and spoke life: I come to You as a woman acquainted with the loneliness of darkness and yet, with its unlimited possibilities.

God, my God, I come having been rejected by the world in which our foremothers birthed, nurtured from their breasts, and set free the children of the oppressors as well as their own. So, it is in Your presence God, and in the company of my sisters, that I receive the "balm of acceptance" that heals our wounds.

Too many of us have been called names that demonize our blackness. We have been denied opportunities, and are pushed to the margins, because of white supremacy and its oppressive systems that were and continue to be legitimized with the fictitious notion of manifest destiny. We are sisters bearing the wounds and battle scars inflicted on the journey for simply being a woman of color—black women living in the tension of doing life and ministry under the dark and heavy cloud of patriarchal misogyny.

My physical, mental, and even spiritual pains are ever before me. Nevertheless I thank You, God, for the liberating testimony of the scars left behind, for they point to Your glory and Your power to deliver. God, I know that they point to Your never-ending love and mercy for me, because I am still here!

Glorious God, I come interceding with thanksgiving for Your life-giving breath that gives us all that has been withheld. May the creative power of Your spirit refresh our souls and renew our minds. Teach us to tend forever to our own gardens. How lovely You are, oh God, and lovely we are, because Your image dwells within. Amen.

Dr. Valerie Carter Smith, Executive Director/Treasurer of the Woman's Missionary Union of Virginia, and

ATTORNEY RHONDA JOY MCLEAN

Prayers For Our Sisters- Call and Response: Creative Economics and Leadership

"I entreat Eu-o'dia and I entreat Syn'tyche to agree in the Lord."

(Philippians 4:2)

This call and response reading can be read as a litany of thanksgiving, community, and proclamation:

Leader: Oh, come, let us welcome and celebrate our abundance in the Lord! Let us celebrate our abundance of love, friendship, and family, however we may define them.

Group: Let us welcome and celebrate our abundance in the Lord.

Leader: Let us celebrate our abundance of resources, whether they take the form of spiritual support, nature's beauty, the friendship of Sisterhood, the material things we want and need, or our inner fortitude and faith.

Group: Let us welcome and celebrate our abundance in the Lord.

Leader: Let us celebrate our ability to Grow in(to) Grace. Even where we may disagree, may we seek to always Listen with Love.

Group: Let us welcome and celebrate our abundance in the Lord.

Leader: Let us celebrate ourselves as women who are called into ministry in its various forms. Let us embrace one another in our spiritual calling and remain open to our Divine purposes and missions.

Group: Let us welcome and celebrate our abundance in the Lord.

Leader: Let us dispel any notions of unworthiness. We are worthy of God's favor, and of a miraculous life we may be unable to imagine.

Group: Let us welcome and celebrate our abundance in the Lord.

Leader: Let us celebrate our intelligence and our unique gifts and talents. However, we are called, wherever we are along our life's journey, we have much to offer to others. Let us embrace our abilities and be grateful for them.

Group: Let us welcome and celebrate our abundance in the Lord.

Leader: Let us love and care for our beings and carefully steward our personal spaces, always taking care of ourselves to be refreshed and renewed.

Group: Let us welcome and celebrate our abundance in the Lord. AMEN.

 Rhonda Joy McLean is the President and CEO of RJMLEADS LLC, a leadership consulting and career advancement

EPILOGUE

ELDER DR. TIFFANY STUBBS

I RISE

This piece was inspired by the sistering of the ATL/ITC RISE Cohort that provided space for me to become…

I breathe,

    I share,

        I dared to leave

            and cared to stay.

I was seen….

    I have been heard,

        I have cried,

           And sighed,

I found a space where I found courage.

I have experienced the metaphysical lap of mothers, aunts, grandmothers, sisters ---

    legs who have walked the places where I want to go;

Thighs that emboldened them to run,

Arms that came back to tell me I can go on.

Hands that have worked and wrote:

Words that have given me life.

I have smiled,

    And laughed,

        Questioned and doubted,

            But always have been reminded,

And was encouraged to be:

   Feminine and free,

   Free and feminine,

    Faith and my femininity are me,

And I am she,

Not afraid to be unapologetically sexy,

Walking in my own intentionality,

Beautiful and bold no matter how I'm dressed.

I have rested,

   I have breathed,

      I have danced into my liberation,

         I have found my place of cultivation.

My legs have been strengthened,

My head has been raised,

I have redefined myself,

And I RISE beyond the ashes…

I RISE far beyond patriarchy,

And hegemony

I RISE to see,

Everything so succinctly,

I am a designer original,

Uniquely me,

I RISE!